The Educator's Guide to Writing a Book

D0139455

The Educator's Guide to Writing a Book is for educators who dream of sharing their knowledge and skills with a broader audience. This exciting resource provides step-by-step guidance on how to set publishing goals, create well-written content and resource material, develop an informative yet accessible writing style, prepare professional-level manuscripts, and anticipate each stage in the publishing process. Chapters include authentic writing examples, tips from veteran authors and publishing professionals, and supportive resources. *The Educator's Guide to Writing a Book* is an invaluable guide that helps aspiring and novice authors move publishing goals from dreams to reality.

Cathie E. West has forty-three years of experience as an educator. She has served as a principal, directed special programs at schools, coordinated curriculum and staff development in school districts, and taught at the college level. West's writing has appeared in many education publications and she is the author of four books.

The Educator's Guide to Writing a Book

Practical Advice for Teachers and Leaders

Cathie E. West

Routledge
Taylor & Francis Group

NEW YORK AND LONDON

First published 2016
by Routledge
711 Third Avenue, New York, NY 10017

and by Routledge
2 Park Square, Milton Park, Abingdon, Oxon, OX14 4RN

Routledge is an imprint of the Taylor & Francis Group, an informa business

© 2016 Taylor & Francis

Library of Congress Cataloging in Publication Data
West, Cathie E.
  The educator's guide to writing a book : practical advice for teachers and
  leaders / Cathie E. West.
    pages cm
  Includes bibliographical references and index.
  1. Education—Authorship—Handbooks, manuals, etc.   2. Educational
  publishing—Handbooks, manuals, etc.   3. Teachers as authors.   I. Title.
  LB1033.5.W47 2016
  371.102'2—dc23   2015011671

ISBN: 978-1-138-82894-0 (hbk)
ISBN: 978-1-138-82895-7 (pbk)
ISBN: 978-1-315-73796-6 (ebk)

Typeset in Optima
by Keystroke, Station Road, Codsall, Wolverhampton

Printed and bound in the United States of America by Publishers Graphics, LLC on sustainably sourced paper.

For Elaine McEwan-Adkins

Contents

Contents

About the Author

Cathie E. West has an MS degree in education and forty-three years of experience as an educator—including thirty-six as a school administrator. Professional responsibilities have included serving as a principal, directing special programs, coordinating curriculum and staff development, and teaching at the college level. Cathie received the Washington Distinguished Principal Award as the representative from Douglas County in 1998, and as the representative from Snohomish County in 2005. She also merited the Leadership for Student Achievement Award from the Washington Association of School Administrators in 2009. In 2010, Mountain Way—the school Cathie led from 2002 to 2013—was designated a School of Distinction by the Center for Educational Effectiveness in collaboration with Phi Delta Kappa (Washington Chapter). Other activities include serving as an editorial adviser for the National Association of Elementary School Principals (2002–5), Washington State Kappan (2007–13), and the Association of Washington School Principals (2011–13). Books include *The 6 Keys to Teacher Engagement: Unlocking the Doors to Top Teacher Performance* (Routledge, 2013); *Problem-Solving Tools and Tips for School Leaders* (Routledge, 2011); and *Leadership Teaming: The Superintendent–Principal Relationship* (Corwin Press, 2009), which was co-authored with Dr. Mary Lynne Derrington. Besides books, Cathie's writing has appeared in *Washington Principal* (AWSP), *Washington State Kappan* (PDK), *Principal* (NAESP), *Communicator* (NAESP), and *ERS Spectrum*. She can be reached at: cathieeileenwest@gmail.com.

Preface

Shortly after my third birthday I noticed the symbols called "print" in story books I could not yet read. Intrigued, I began filling up scrap paper with indecipherable scribbles that I proudly referred to as writing. Alphabet savvy by age five, I could print my name; copy important words like "mother," "Christmas," and "birthday"; and hammer out childhood fantasies, such as "*I cn rid mi bik to the mooon.*" Throughout elementary school I explored writing through voracious reading, plowing through my town library's books for kids, the family encyclopedia set, and my great-aunt's ancient *Reader's Digest* collection. Although my reading world was limited when I was young, it mushroomed when I hit secondary school and college. I took every literature class I could cram into my busy schedules and my appreciation for the power of writing deepened.

My confidence in the written word continued after starting my career in education. When overwhelmed by the problems associated with teaching and student learning, I turned to books for help and found solutions in the practical guides written by more experienced educators. Once I became a principal—and my responsibilities soared—I pored over books by Michael Fullan, Thomas Guskey, Carl Glickman, Robert Marzano, and Elaine McEwan, to name just a few. Their compelling narratives delivered fresh ideas, eye-opening research findings, and uplifting stories from the field.

I eventually moved from reading other educators' writing to writing for other educators. I began my literary journey by submitting "how to" articles to professional magazines. Although the topics were not particularly complex, these short professional "essays" brought positive feedback from other educators. Encouraged, I delved into richer topics for articles and these also elicited appreciative messages. Writing books was the logical next step and the affirmation I have received from my readers has been powerful.

Why I Wrote This Book

I am not the most experienced education writer publishing today; nor do I view myself as a writing "expert." On the other hand, every book proposal I have submitted to major publishers has been readily accepted and every book I have been contracted to write has been successfully completed. So why am I writing this book? Like many educators, I am driven to help others. I received encouragement when I began writing and now it is my turn to support new writers. I had no map to follow when I began writing books for educators; the steps I followed evolved over time. Now, with four published books on the shelves, I can offer a map—a time-tested map—to the readers of this book. My only hope is that *The Educator's Guide to Writing a Book* empowers you to write your own!

What You Will Find

You will find credible advice from experienced educators, writers, and publishing professionals; step-by-step book development instructions; and practical resources. The following chapter snapshots will help guide your reading:

- Chapter 1 explores reasons to write, common misconceptions about writing, critical attributes of successful authors, and goal setting. You will learn how to identify your book's purpose, assess the qualities you bring to the writing process, and set personal goals that will positively impact your writing proficiency.
- Chapter 2 surveys the characteristics of popular education books— high-interest topics, appealing writing styles, and practical information. You will learn how to assess the quality of books written for teachers and school leaders and identify the features you want to incorporate into your own book.

- Chapter 3 covers the elements that make up the main text of a book and the items that appear at the front and back. You will learn how to access publishers' submission and writing guidelines, determine which reference books to acquire, create an author's biography, identify desirable text features and images, and keep your manuscript secure.

- Chapter 4 focuses upon title, topic, and theme development; education issue alignment; and the preparation of book proposal documents. You will learn how to choose an enticing theme, generate supporting topics, develop an effective title, and prepare a quality prospectus and submission letter.

- Chapter 5 delves into writing style, process actions that support non-fiction writing, and book development steps. You will learn how to acquire an appealing writing style, develop chapter content, and prepare your manuscript—from title page to bibliography.

- Chapter 6 discusses book contract considerations, the responsibilities of publishing personnel, steps in the publishing process, and marketing strategies. You will learn how to work with editors and production team members, code your book's special features correctly, submit a properly prepared manuscript, and support marketing efforts.

Special Features

- Interviews: Informative Q&As with experienced writers, educators, and publishing professionals.

- Author's Notes: Authentic stories and suggestions that will enhance your publishing experience.

- Take Away Tips: Concise summaries of major concepts and suggestions.

- Reflections–Connections: Thought-provoking questions that promote self-reflection, career connections, and personal growth.

- Best Practice: Activities that will help you apply new concepts and skills.

- Resources Available as Free Downloads: Implementation tools—templates, checklists, and sample documents—can be found in the Appendices and at www.routledge.com/9781138828957.

Whom This Book Is For

Potential readers—and authors—include elementary and secondary teachers; school principals; directors of curriculum, instruction, and special programs; and superintendents and their cadres of assistants. The targeted audience also includes university instructors offering courses that pertain to education, writing, and publishing.

How to Use This Book

The Educators Guide to Writing a Book: Practical Advice for Teachers and Leaders is an ideal book development guide for aspiring authors. It can also serve as a practical reference for writing workshops, book studies, and university courses. Whether selected for individual self-study or used as an instructional tool, it is beneficial to read the chapters in order, since the concepts presented evolve sequentially. Readers will also get more from the book by responding to the Reflection–Connection questions and completing the Best Practice activities.

Acknowledgements

Elaine McEwan-Adkins has had an extraordinary impact on the field of education. She has been an inspiring and award-winning teacher, principal, and district-level administrator—but that's not all. Elaine is an accomplished author whose superbly crafted books have strengthened professional practice at all levels. She is also a generous mentor to new writers. For example, Elaine graciously agreed to share her writing expertise with the readers of this book, and I am grateful—as I am sure you will be—for her enlightening commentary.

Two other talented educators, principal Bob Busk and teacher Robyn Ross, contributed their professional experience and wisdom to this book. You will appreciate their reality-based remarks and delightful observations.

Priceless support was also provided by my exceptional editor, Heather Jarrow, whose high standards, publishing expertise, and spot-on advice powered up the quality of this book. I am also indebted to the following publishing professionals for sharing their inside view of publishing: Karen Adler, Lauren Beebe, Lauren Davis, Samuel Huber, Laurie Lieb, Bob Sickles, and Amy Vanderzee.

Resources Available as Free Downloads

Access: www.routledge.com/9781138828957:

- Appendix A: Reasons to Write
- Appendix B: Writing Goals Form
- Appendix C: Book Analysis Guide
- Appendix D: Author Bio Template
- Appendix E: Chapter Text and Images Worksheet
- Appendix F: Sample Query Letter
- Appendix G: Sample Prospectus
- Appendix H: Sample Submission Letter
- Appendix I: Chapter Framework and Features Template
- Appendix J: Sample Manuscript Submission Checklist

1 Why Write?

[W]riters live their lives differently because they write.

Lucy McCormick Calkins with Shelley Harwayne (1991, p. 7)

Thinking about writing a book? Good for you! If you pursue this commendable goal you will not only make a contribution to your field but embark upon a mentally stimulating, highly creative, and professionally rewarding adventure, one *The Educator's Guide to Writing a Book* will support—step by step—from title page to index and all points in between. Perhaps, however, you have already penned a manuscript for a book but failed to place it with a publisher. Should that be the case, this book is also for you. The tips, examples, and resources in this chapter, and those that follow, should help your publishing dreams become a reality. But before launching into book preparation details, we'll take a look at the reasons why teachers and school leaders should set aside time to write.

Reasons to Write

Although writing a book may seem overwhelming, there are powerful reasons for beginning this breathtaking journey. The most compelling drivers—to serve, to lead, to teach, and to inspire—are presented below, with several examples of recently published books.

To Serve

Sharing information—ideas, experiences, skills, research—that helps educators become more proficient is a valuable way to serve others. A book is the ideal communication vehicle for "sharing" since it has the potential to reach a wide audience. *Applying Servant Leadership in Today's Schools* by Mary Culver (2009) exemplifies the type of book that "serves" practitioners. Culver presents service leadership strategies coupled with authentic scenarios that support their implementation.

To Lead

Professionals in the vanguard of leading-edge educational practices often write books that show others how to follow along. A case in point is Richard and Rebecca DuFour and Robert Eaker. This influential trio has written extensively about the role professional learning communities (PLCs) play in improving teachers' effectiveness. In *Revisiting Professional Learning Communities at Work: New Insights for Improving Schools* (DuFour et al., 2008) PLC principles are reviewed along with strategies for breaking down barriers that impede their implementation.

To Teach

The desire to "teach" provides another reason to write. Robert Marzano, for example, has authored a series of books that introduces educators to research-based practices that strengthen instructional outcomes. Among the best is *Formative Assessment and Standards-Based Grading: Classroom Strategies that Work*, which includes step-by-step assessment instructions and valuable evaluation tools (Marzano, 2010).

Another example of books that "teach" is provided by *Teaching the iGeneration: 5 Easy Ways to Introduce Essential Skills with Web 2.0 Tools* by Ferriter and Garry (2010). From this up to the minute tech resource teachers learn how to use websites, blogs, wikis, videos, Skype, podcasts, and other Web 2.0 tools to enrich instructional presentations.

To Inspire

Sometimes achieving educational goals seems impossible, especially with setbacks like test scores that sink instead of soar, students who fail instead of flourish, and faculty members who evade rather than embrace challenges. It is no wonder that a discouraged school leader would grab hold of *The Moral Imperative of School Leadership* by Michael Fullan (2003). Although a slim volume, this book packs a punch aimed at revitalizing the principalship through collaborative cultures, shared leadership, and purposeful behavior. It "inspires" by sharing specific strategies for managing change paired with credible stories of leadership success.

Now that you have reviewed the four rationales for preparing a book, use the Reasons to Write worksheet (Appendix A) to identify the motivators that apply to you. If there are additional reasons why you are considering writing a book, be sure to jot them down.

Reasons *Not* to Write

Although the intent of this book is to fuel your authorship ambitions, to be fair, let's take a look at reasons *not* to write a book. There are a few myths about the rewards that come from publishing that ought to be dispelled. So take note: educators should not write a book for any of the following reasons.

For Money

Some inexperienced authors picture hefty monetary rewards from publishing a book. The truth is that the remuneration will be modest, and that's only if the book sells in considerable numbers, not just at first but over the long haul. There are also expenses associated with writing a book, such as buying a computer, word-processing software, copy paper, and printer ink. Reference books and subscriptions to online professional journals cost money too, so that has to be included in the literary budget. Writing time should also be factored in. What do you earn per hour?

If you spend twenty hours a week writing, what does that add up to—at your normal hourly rate—over the span of a year or more? The truth is that writing an education book, although immensely satisfying, will not make the author tons of money. On the other hand, if the book is touted by the latest television guru, endorsed by a sports celebrity, or becomes the basis for a blockbuster film, maybe the author *will* strike gold!

For Approval

Do you crave affirmation for the job you perform? Are you crushed when you encounter disapproval? Does being evaluated unnerve you? If you answer "yes" to any of these questions, you will need to toughen up before publishing a book. No matter how much thought and time you devote to the development of your manuscript, during the publishing process you can expect criticism—albeit *constructive* criticism—from your editor, manuscript reviewers, and copy editor. And once the book is published you may encounter individuals who just flat out do not like your book (just pray that it is not a reviewer for a major publication). But you should not lose heart because there are people you *can* count on for unconditional approval—your family. Not only will family members love your book; they will purchase multiple copies!

For Career Advancement

Listing a published book on your résumé is guaranteed to catch the eye of a potential employer but no one is going to hire you simply because you are an author. You will climb the career ladder because of your talents, reputation, and compatibility with job requirements. This proviso also applies to professors who are pressured to publish in order to attain tenure. At higher education institutions, publishing is not the sole determinant that governs professorial advancement.

Have your hopes been dashed by the foregoing review of publishing myths? Probably not, since few educators write books for personal gain. So, assuming your interest in book writing is still solidly intact, the critical attributes that are necessary for bringing your book project to fruition follow.

Author Attributes

Anyone who takes on the impressive responsibilities associated with writing a book should be *confident, committed, conscientious*, and *courageous*. Don't feel intimidated by these prize-winning traits, however, because if you are a successful educator you already have these essential attributes. If you are a teacher, for example, you are confident about the subject matter you teach, committed to meeting the needs of your students, conscientious about carrying out your assigned duties, and courageous when circumventing serious trouble, such as "out of control" students who strike out at others.

Likewise, principals are confident about overseeing the operation of their schools, committed to raising every student's achievement, conscientious about fulfilling their legal responsibilities, and courageous when managing emergencies, such as school "lockdowns" precipitated by threatening intruders.

But how do these four attributes apply to writing?

Confident

Authors find out where their talents lie from editorial and readership feedback. Writers may learn, for example, that they are A+ organizational engineers, word-choice wizards, or punctuation prodigies. Nevertheless, when problems are identified—spelling snafus, grammar glitches, metaphor mix-ups—authors *remain* confident that they can learn what they do not yet know how to do and put it into practice in their writing.

Committed

Book writing is pure joy. Finding the perfect quote for a chapter lead-in, composing a sentence that captures the essence of an elusive concept, and generating narratives that flow effortlessly across the page are satisfying accomplishments. But since the time it takes to prepare a book may span more than a year, authorship requires a fair amount of commitment. To craft a product as complex as a book requires daily, weekly, and monthly attention. Does this sound onerous? Relax! If you have successfully prepared lengthy end-of-term reports for graduate-level courses, a master's thesis, or a doctoral dissertation, you already possess the level of commitment necessary to see a book through to completion.

Conscientious

There are numerous details associated with writing a book, such as following conventional grammar, spelling, and punctuation rules; coding text boxes, tables, and images sequentially; and identifying research sources with accurate text-embedded citations and bibliographic notations. A newbie author soon learns that writing about a worthy theme, although highly significant, is just one of their responsibilities; a meticulous approach to manuscript preparation is just as critical. Fortunately, educators attend to details on a daily basis, so meticulousness is not a foreign performance characteristic. To reinforce this, there are numerous resources in the chapters that follow that will help creative writers become *conscientious* writers.

Courageous

How do you feel about having your writing scrutinized—not just by your editor but by manuscript reviewers, copy editors, and production staff members. Once your book is published, your writing will also be examined by the people who have bought it; by your family, friends, and colleagues; and by journalists who are assigned to review it for professional publications. Scary? Not if you keep in mind that feedback—especially critical feedback—helps you grow as a writer. You will also find that you will take the evaluation of your writing in your stride as you gain authorship experience.

Writing in a confident, committed, conscientious, and courageous manner is achievable for any successful educator. All it takes is recognizing —and celebrating—one's talents and setting goals to strengthen perceived weaknesses. The information that follows will support self-assessment activities.

Writing Proficiency Goals

The first step in the book development process should be an honest appraisal of what you *know*, what you can *do*, and what you should *learn*.

To guide your self-evaluation, the attributes of a well-prepared writer follow. As you review each characteristic, jot down your writing proficiency objectives in the Writing Goals Form (Appendix B).

Stays Professionally up to Date

Educators must stay current to write knowledgeably about their profession, and reading is an efficient way to learn about new developments. There are countless print and online resources available, such as: *Phi Delta Kappan* (www.pdkintl.org), a highly respected periodical with an international perspective; *Education Week* (www.edweek.org), an up to the minute news source; and ASCD (www.ascd.org), a leading professional organization offering a wide range of education books, articles, commentary, and staff development opportunities. Another rich information source is Websites for Educators (www.gse.harvard.edu/educator_ resources), where you will find over 400 links to worldwide websites covering a potpourri of topics, including elementary and secondary school curricula, higher education policies, school and district-level leadership, and education reform.

Attending major education conferences is another way to stay up to date. If professional travel funds are scarce, however, join blogs like The Innovative Educator (www.theinnovativeeducator.blogspot.com) and Mind Shift (www.blogs.kqed.org/mindshift.about). Blogs provide an easy way to make contact with colleagues and keep abreast of education developments. To "blog-on," enter "top education blogs" into a search engine and countless sites will pop up for your consideration. Choose the blogs that are sponsored by organizations, news sources, and agencies you trust.

If you have fallen behind in your professional reading, set a goal to cruise print and online sources each day. This will be easy if you read during the spare minutes that are available during coffee breaks, between meetings, or while waiting for appointments.

Reads Practitioner Books

If writing for teachers and school leaders seems intimidating, find out how other writers have approached this mission. Start by reviewing the education books—not textbooks, but reader-friendly practical guides—offered by major publishers, such as those listed in the box below.

- Corwin Press (www.corwin.com)
- Guilford Press (www.guilford.com)
- Heinemann (www.heinemann.com)
- Jossey-Bass/Wiley (www.josseybass.com)
- Routledge (www.routledge.com)
- Solution Tree (www.solution-tree.com)
- Stenhouse Publishers (www.stenhouse.com)

Select a few books to peruse, taking note of the writing styles, content organization, chapter layouts, and text features, such as headings, graphics, photos, tables, and charts. Read the narratives carefully, too; you should find that the writing is more akin to a conversational magazine article than to the formal writing associated with academic publications. If you have favorite authors, what do you like about their books? Perhaps there are stories that breathe life into the author's suggestions, research references that lend credibility to the writer's assertions, or maybe "reflection" questions that help you identify with the author's opinions. Eventually, your vision of the perfect book will evolve.

If you need to do more professional reading, select a chapter from a variety of books to review each week. As you read, use a highlighter to identify the features that enhance the book's appeal. Perhaps you should incorporate the qualities you admire into *your* book, too.

Strengthens Writing Skills

Most educators consider themselves competent writers since they are regularly called upon to produce bulletins, handbooks, plans, applications, newsletters, agendas, correspondence, reports, and the like. But this type of writing may or may not be done skillfully or prepare a teacher or principal to create an appealing narrative for a book. To assess your own writing acumen, consider taking the following test:

- Part I: Using the active voice, write a fluent, reader-friendly essay about a favorite subject. The supporting ideas, word choice, tone, and sentence structure should align with the topic and strengthen the narrative. In addition, sentences should illustrate the effective use of parallel construction, subject–verb and noun–pronoun agreement, prepositions, adjectives, adverbs, and dependent and independent clauses. Above all else, make this piece interesting!
- Part II: Write sentences that demonstrate appropriate usage of the apostrophe, comma, colon, dash, ellipsis, exclamation point, hyphen, parenthesis, period, question mark, and semi-colon.

If you were not intimidated by this writing assessment, you already have the basic writing skills nailed down. But don't fret if you found it perplexing. You probably use all of the elements highlighted in Part I of the assessment in your writing but have forgotten their names. Learning the proper terminology for and usage of grammatical features will heighten your awareness of how these components work to enhance sentence fluency and interest. As for the punctuation quiz, few writers have problems with routine writing marks, such as the apostrophe and parenthesis. When to use the comma and semi-colon, however, has left more than a few writers shaking their heads. Then there are the dashes, ellipses, and hyphens to worry about! If you feel you need grammar and punctuation brush-ups, check out literary websites like GrammarBook.com (http://grammarbook. com) and The Writing Center at the University of North Carolina (http:// writingcenter.unc.edu/files/2012/09/Style-TheWriting-Center.pdf).

Creates the "Right" Writing Environment

Do you long for a dream writing location? Perhaps a sunny island in the South Seas; a lavish Mediterranean cruise ship; or a Parisian sidewalk café crawling with likeminded artists? The reality is that the *right* writing environment can be found in your own home. Being a wordsmith requires only a place to work, such as a guest room, an attic alcove, or a kitchen nook. As for accoutrements, these are simple: a well-lit writing surface, a

Author's Note about Viewpoint

Life changes when you write books. I notice details in books that would have escaped my notice prior to publishing. Take *Raising Chickens for Dummies*, a handy livestock reference I acquired because I live on a farm with—you guessed it—chickens (Willis and Ludlow, 2009). The narrative is written in the *second person* (to "you"), and since my new poultry guide is exceptionally reader-friendly, I am left wondering: "Should I try using the second person in *my* writing?"

I did not pay much attention to this first–second–third person business when I took literature classes in school, but now, because I see myself as a writer, I think about viewpoint and how it impacts the reader. A while back, I learned that the blockbuster memoir *All Creatures Great and Small*, written by the veterinarian Alf Wight (aka James Herriot), did not find a publisher until the stories were shifted from the third person (about he–she–it) to the first person (from the viewpoint of "I"). That was an astonishing revelation (Lord, 1997)! By taking note of an obscure literary fact like this, I continue to grow as a writer.

comfortable chair, a computer with internet access, a fast printer, and the usual office supplies.

Arranging the physical environment, however, is just the start. For your book project to go smoothly you will need your family's support. When you need time to write—especially when running up against a publishing deadline—household members should pick up some of your responsibilities and give you uninterrupted writing time. Discuss the assistance you will need with the people who share your home. You will probably find that they are eager to help.

Makes Connections

Writing is energizing when you connect with kindred spirits. Get to know other writers by attending writers' conferences or joining an online literary chat group. Another approach is to locate a mentor who is willing to provide guidance. Tracking down an experienced writer isn't as hard as it might sound, since most authors provide contact information with the articles and books they publish. You could also be bold and initiate a writers' support group in the region where you live.

Q&A with Robyn Ross, Elementary Teacher

Robyn Ross is a bright, energetic, full-time first-grade teacher who typifies the aspiring education writer. Her life was jam-packed *before* adding a book to her plate. Robyn is an exemplary teacher, highly involved instructional leader, and much sought-after curriculum developer at Mountain Way, an elementary school in the wilds of Snohomish County, Washington. When she is not working, Robyn manages the home front and cares for Zeke—a lively tyke recently adopted from China. Zeke, who is described as a "dynamo," keeps Robyn on her toes. In her not so spare time, Robyn helps her husband, who is also fully employed, with the renovation of a Victorian-era house. In the interview that follows, Robyn discusses the push to write and the difficulties that arise from weaving writing into her work-filled world.

Cathie: You have gotten your publishing feet wet by contributing your thoughts to books written by Elaine McEwan-Adkins, a popular education writer, and to articles and books that I have written. What have you learned?

Robyn: As silly as it sounds, I learned that people might be interested in what I have to say! Writing is a personal outlet so having my words taken seriously by professional writers, and being sought out as a book contributor, has opened my eyes to the potential for more.

Cathie: And now, writing a book of your own has become an important goal. What is your topic and who is your audience?

Robyn: An idea that has intrigued me for some time is a book on writing. My audience would be teachers in the primary grades.

Cathie: What prompted you to choose this topic?

Robyn: I have been teaching for more than fourteen years and have *never* had an adopted set of writing materials to work from—

Teacher Profile: Robyn Ross

Education
BA Interdisciplinary Child Development
MA Education with Reading Endorsement—Western Washington University

Current Position
First-Grade Teacher—Mountain Way Elementary, Granite Falls, Washington

Awards
School of Distinction Teacher 2010

Leadership Activities
Professional Learning Community Teacher Leader
Transforming Professional Learning Committee Member

First-Grade Curriculum Writing
Student Friendly Learning Targets for Writing, Reading, Math
Science Scope and Sequence
Student–Parent Homework Contracts

Publishing Experience
(See References for full titles, issue dates, and publishers)
Quoted in:
Elaine K. McEwan, *10 Traits of Highly Effective Schools*
Cathie E. West and Lois Frank, *Climbing Higher*
Cathie E. West, *The 6 Keys to Teacher Engagement*

everything I know about teaching writing has come from watching or talking to other teachers. My "dream book" is a resource for K-2 teachers demonstrating how it *is* possible for young children to write in a way that makes sense to *them* while using writing process steps provided by the teacher.

Cathie: Sounds like a dynamite book for any teacher—especially inexperienced ones. What motivates you to take this on?

Robyn: Having a resource that lays out—step by step—a process for moving children forward in writing, along with concrete project ideas and writing samples, is huge! If I can find a way to create such a resource, and tie it to Common Core State Standards, it would benefit me as well as other primary teachers.

Cathie: What is your vision of the writing process?

Robyn: First and foremost, writing should be fun. It shouldn't be stressful or cause students to question their abilities. One of the first things I tell students is that getting their ideas "out of their brains and onto paper" is the most important step in writing. Although I need to focus on handwriting, spelling, punctuation, sentence structure, and specific types of writing for grading purposes, those are secondary to students getting something on paper. Students who are afraid of being "wrong" usually choose not to write.

Cathie: First-graders are just beginning to read and write; how do you get them to jot down their ideas?

Robyn: We create story maps using quick pictures that allow students to produce ideas without having to write a word. This is similar to outlining where you want to go when writing an article, academic paper, or book.

Cathie: What's next?

Robyn: Each idea is expanded into sentence form. I model how to reread what has been written to make sure it makes sense, use editing marks, and insert more information. Once rough drafts are completed, students conference with me individually and we edit their work together. During this conference we look for correct punctuation and clarity of ideas. Details can be added during this conversation if either of us feels there is something missing. My students learn how to turn a rough draft into a quality final draft.

Cathie: The writing steps you take with students also work for adults.

Robyn: My steps are similar to what authors do as they start writing the "meat" of their text and turn their outlines into something more tangible.

Cathie: I can tell you are excited about your book but it is still in the planning stages. What barriers to writing have you run into?

> ## Best Writing Tip
>
> Write when you can, because you never know when you will have a chance again!
>
> Robyn Ross, first-grade teacher

Robyn: Time, or more accurately the lack of time, is the initial barrier. Working full time, having a toddler running loose, working at home on school tasks that workday minutes don't cover, and making sure that my home, husband, and child are taken care of all limit my time to write.

Cathie: What other barriers are out there?

Robyn: Motivation is a barrier that presents itself like a brick wall. When I have time to write I lack the motivation and when I have the motivation to write time may not be available. Zeke's naptime offers quiet time for completing tasks but my "to do" list is usually longer than the minutes of quiet. When my school and home obligations are met—and my son has not stirred—I find myself unmotivated to tackle the task of writing a book. This is when I decompress by sitting on the porch swing, reading a good book written by someone else.

Cathie: I think many writers understand your dilemma. Writing a book can feel overwhelming.

Robyn: Definitely! Getting started is daunting and not helped by my insecurities. Where do I start? Can I do this? Am I going to be able to accomplish this task with any measure of success? The idea of tackling a project of this magnitude, putting time, energy, and effort into it and then having it be unsuccessful is a scary proposition.

Cathie: And yet you still are driven to write this book.

Robyn: Yes. When looked at individually, time, motivation, and insecurity are barriers I can overcome.

Cathie: How will you do that?

Robyn: Setting up a support system is key. I know I work well when I have a schedule in place for what needs to be accomplished.

Once a schedule is set it is also helpful to be held accountable by an outside entity—my husband, a co-worker, my principal.

Cathie: Anything else?

Robyn: I need to believe in myself, trust my abilities, and get to work!

Although a fresh-from-the-box writer, Robyn exhibits the "can do" spirit that underlies the successful completion of any book. She takes note of the obstacles that impede writing opportunities but is not intimidated by them. Robyn also understands that creating a solid support system is as important as the content of her writing guide. Is there a published book in Robyn's future? Absolutely!

Take Away Tips

- Education books contribute by serving, leading, teaching, and inspiring other professionals to do their best work.

- Book writing is a rewarding journey that promotes personal and professional development.

- Authors are confident they can learn what they do not know and put new skills into practice in their writing.

- It takes commitment to write a book, the kind of commitment that successful educators bring to their work every day.

- Conscientious writers are not just creative; they attend to the numerous details associated with preparing their manuscripts for publication.

- Feedback—especially critical feedback—helps writers grow.

- A well-prepared education writer reads a wide range of professional books, strengthens writing skills, and creates a supportive writing environment.

- Connections with other writers provide enriching literary experiences.

Reflections–Connections

- Think about the academic papers and professional documents you have prepared throughout your education and career. Can any of this material enrich the theme you have chosen for your new book?

- Are you confident, committed, conscientious, and courageous? What personal qualities do you need to develop further to become a successful writer? What steps will you take to make this happen?

Best Practice

- Choose a location in your home for writing and gather the furnishings and equipment you will need, such as a good desk and chair, computer and printer, office supplies, shelves for reference books, and a file cabinet (or crate) for document folders. Discuss your writing needs with family members. Will they actively support your project? In what ways?

- Find another writer—through your place of work, social network, or professional organization—with whom you can share writing goals and challenges. How will you support each other's work?

References

Culver, M. K. (2009). *Applying servant leadership in today's schools.* New York: Routledge

Dufour, R., DuFour, R., and Eaker, R. (2008). *Revisiting professional learning communities at work: New insights for improving schools.* Bloomington, IN: Solution Tree Press

Ferriter, W. M. and Garry, A. (2010). *Teaching the iGeneration: 5 easy ways to introduce essential skills with Web 2.0 tools.* Bloomington, IN: Solution Tree Press

Fullan, M. (2003). *The moral imperative of school leadership.* Thousand Oaks, CA: Corwin Press

Lord, Graham. (1997). *James Herriot: The life of a country vet.* New York: Carroll & Graf

Marzano, R. (2010). *Formative assessment and standards-based grading: Classroom strategies that work.* Bloomington, IN: Solution Tree Press

McCormick Calkins, L. with Harwayne, S. (1991). *Living between lines.* Portsmouth, NH: Heinemann

McEwan, E. K. (2009). *10 traits of highly effective schools: Raising the achievement bar for all students.* Thousand Oaks, CA: Corwin Press

West, C. E. (2013). *The 6 keys to teacher engagement: Unlocking the doors to top teacher performance.* New York: Routledge

West, C. E. and Frank, L. (2010). Climbing higher: Mountain Way Elementary. *Washington State Kappan,* 4(2), 18–21

Willis, K. and Ludlow, R. (2009). *Raising chickens for dummies.* Hoboken, NJ: Wiley

2

Best-Practice Practitioner Books

Fear of writing is the terrifying feeling that somehow no one will ever read what you have written, or they will read it and reject it. It takes a few books to gain that confidence in one's voice and to believe that if people actually buy what you are "selling" they will be more effective educators.

Elaine McEwan-Adkins

What do teachers and school leaders want from a professional book? Attend a major education symposium, like the Assessment Training Institute's Summer Conference (http://ati.pearson.com) or ASCD's Annual Conference and Exhibit Show (http://ascd.org), and spend an hour or two wandering around the book display aisles. By listening to the conversations of other visitors, noting the books that are picked up for perusal, and seeing which volumes are actually purchased, you will tap into the book-buying preferences of teachers and school leaders. The conversations you overhear will go something like this:

Teacher: This book about managing disruptive students looks great! There are lots of practical techniques.
Principal: Here's a book about personnel problems that I could have used yesterday. It covers the lack of professionalism which is a recurring problem at my school.
Curriculum director: At last, a book about how *kids* are impacted by assessment changes. The author has a step-by-step process for helping students make adjustments.
Superintendent: I need a book to boost principal morale and I think this is it. There are case studies about successful schools and leadership strategies that make sense.

It should be no surprise that the individual needs of teachers and administrators underlie their book-buying interests. And responding to readership "interests" is exactly what a best-practice practitioner book should do. But given that a book takes a year or more to produce, how do writers predict what readers' *future* interests will be?

Interest Assessment Variables

Although a crystal ball is always an option, there are better ways to determine the future interests of book buyers. These include drawing upon one's personal experience, reviewing professional standards for teachers and administrators, and keeping abreast of educational trends.

Personal Experience

The most obvious way to gauge readership "wants" is to draw upon one's own professional experience. Former teachers, for example, know from working in the trenches that student discipline will always be a top topic for other teachers. Likewise, veteran principals know that personnel management will head the book-buying list for school leaders. But since writers' experiences are limited to what *they* have encountered—and these encounters may not be representative—authors should look beyond their personal realms and consider additional approaches.

Teacher Standards

Professional standards, which describe what practitioners are required to *know* and *do*, provide another way to learn about the concerns of educators. A reliable source for teacher competencies is the National Board for Professional Teaching Standards (www.nbpts.org), which identifies such responsibilities as maintaining a commitment to serving students, strengthening subject knowledge, guiding students effectively, growing professionally, and collaborating with colleagues and families (NBPTS, 2002). A wealth of potential book themes could be derived from the expectations listed in the standards. In regards to student commitment, for example, cultural sensitivity, student motivation, and character development are just a few of the subjects that come to mind.

Administrative Competencies

For school administrators, the "go to" source for professional competencies is the *Interstate School Leaders Licensure Consortium Standards (ISLLC)*. The current version, the *Educational Leadership Policy Standards*, covers six domains: shared vision, school culture, organizational management, collaboration, professional behavior, and social–political–cultural awareness (CCSSO, 2008). Within each domain are "must have" leadership skills that authors writing for administrators would be wise to consider. "Shared vision" alone could generate a boatload of book themes, such as collaborative leadership, social sensitivity, goal development, and management of the "change" process. The *ISLLC* standards are being updated, however, and the public review draft—the *2014 ISLLC Standards*—was available online from the Council of Chief State School Officers (www.ccsso.org) at the time of writing. Check out the CCSSO website for subsequent drafts and, eventually, the final version.

Instructional Frameworks

Many school districts have adopted teaching "frameworks" that guide the instruction that takes place in elementary and secondary classrooms. Three of the better-known frameworks are listed in the box below.

- The Framework for Teaching: Developed by Charlotte Danielson (www.danielsongroup.org).
- The Marzano Teacher Evaluation Model: Developed by Robert Marzano (www.marzanocenter.com).
- 5 Dimensions of Learning: Developed by the Center for Educational Leadership (CEL) (www.k-12leadership.org).

The Marzano, Danielson, and CEL models specify performance criteria that writers should be cognizant of when crafting instructional recommendations for teachers. Fortunately, there are similarities between these three frameworks—for example, each model addresses effective practices pertaining to student engagement, instruction, and assessment.

Need more information? All three models can be accessed via the Washington Teacher Principal Evaluation Project website (http://tpep-wa.org).

Educational Trends

Educational trends are also reliable predictors of readership interests—as long as the new approaches have staying power. Innovations like ED-TECH (Educational Technology) and STEM (Science–Technology–Engineering–Mathematics Education), for example, appear to have longevity, so books that support these programs should attract audiences for a good many years. To find out what is in vogue, read contemporary books and journals, join professional organizations, and attend major education conferences that showcase high-profile presenters.

Readership Wants

Anyone who has recruited participants for book studies quickly learns what busy educators hope to gain from their professional readings. A promising book helps practitioners improve their performance—and ultimately the performance of their students—and makes their job a good deal easier. To these ends, a best-practice book provides teachers and school leaders with several important assets.

Enlightening Information

When educational initiatives emerge, such as implementing the Common Core State Standards (CCSS) and organizing professional learning communities (PLCs), teachers and school leaders are hungry for information. What is the research behind the new approach? How do school leaders convince teachers to embrace the change? Who can provide staff training? Books that support new initiatives by answering such questions will be in high demand. And books that share successful implementation practices will be even more popular.

Fresh Ideas

New and veteran educators are always on the lookout for better ways to handle their responsibilities. Teachers, for example, want more effective ways to organize classrooms, prepare lesson plans, and access tech resources. Principals also need support, such as strategies to help them handle tight budgets, underperforming personnel, and demanding accountability mandates. And both teachers and leaders want to improve their output and efficiency. Books offering practitioners novel ideas that will make their day-to-day duties less burdensome will have high appeal.

Reliable Research

A best-practice practitioner book shares reliable research from such fields as education, psychology, sociology, medicine, and the neurosciences. But what exactly is "reliable" research? Some educational practices emerge solely from theories about what *might* work in schools; they are never actually field tested in classroom settings. Other theory-derived practices *are* tested, but by way of small clinical studies under controlled conditions, such as lab settings with carefully selected participants. Unfortunately, a controlled lab setting is not an *authentic* setting. The most reliable educational research is more thorough—a proposed practice is given a lengthy trial in "real-life" schools. When the outcomes are positive, educators have confidence that the practices are likely to work (Ellis, 2005). Books that promote practices based upon reliable research will grab the attention of teachers and school leaders.

Solid Solutions

Teachers and principals are inundated with challenges, such as underachieving students, unsupportive communities, and parents who demand too much from their schools and too little from themselves. Books that offer remedies for such problems—not pie in the sky but realistic ones—will attract a receptive audience.

Best-Practice Books Defined

The word "best" has already been used multiple times in this book in conjunction with "practice," but the meaning of these two terms may not be clear. The box below therefore provides definitions that capture their essence.

- Best: Offering or producing the greatest advantage;
- Practice: A repeated or customary action.

(Merriam-Webster, 2008, pp. 118, 974)

Benefits

A best-practice book gives "the greatest advantage" to educators by promoting the acquisition of "actions" that yield beneficial results. A recent example is Terrell's *The 30 Goals Challenge for Teachers: Small Steps to Transform Your Teaching* (2015). This book empowers teachers—and benefits students—by sharing practices that promote positive thinking, self-improvement, collaborative relationships, and quality instruction. Another example is *Insights: How Expert Principals Make Difficult Decisions*, by Dionne V. McLaughlin (2015). School leaders learn data-based problem-solving strategies supported by resources, such as reflection questions and teacher evaluation tools. Some additional attributes that make a best-practice book a must-have book are outlined in Table 2.1.

Attributes

The book characteristics identified in Table 2.1 do not happen by chance. Savvy authors capture these qualities intentionally. In the enlightening interview that follows you will learn more about the development of best-practice books from a highly regarded author.

Table 2.1 Best-Practice Book Attributes

Attribute	Look-fors
Accessible Writing Style	Reader-friendliness characterizes the writing style. The text flows smoothly and is easy to read and understand. There are vivid stories that illustrate important concepts. See Chapter 5
Enticing Topic	The subject matter is of high interest to educators; the content enlightens current issues, offers fresh information, and/or introduces educational innovations. See Chapter 4
Clear Purpose	Lack of clarity is not a problem with this book. The objectives are spelled out in the introduction and referenced as the chapters unfold. See Chapter 4
Useful Content	The "big ideas" are practical and supported by examples, case studies, success stories, activities, reflection questions, quick tips, and process steps. See Chapter 3
Reliable Research, References, and Data	Assertions made by the author are backed up by quality research, meaningful data, and supporting references, such as articles, books, interviews, and surveys from the fields of education, psychology, sociology, medicine, and the neurosciences. See Chapter 5
Multiple Uses	The book is suitable not only for individual reading but also for book studies, workshops, seminars, and college courses. See Chapter 5
Appealing Format and Features	Design elements enhance the book's accessibility. Text features include headings and subheadings, bullet lists, keywords, text boxes, illustrations, labels, and captions. Graphic organizers like charts, webs, maps, diagrams, and timelines serve to clarify concepts. See Chapters 5 and 6
Resources	Resources include downloadable tools like worksheets, forms, quizzes, self-assessments, forms, and surveys. Technological supports include CDs, DVDs, blogs, webinars, website links, and online courses. See Chapter 5

Author's Note about Stories

I grew up on folktales, fables, and fairytales, and the messages conveyed by these vivid vignettes made an indelible impression. So, when I began reading Roland Barth's *Lessons Learned: Shaping Relationships and the Culture in the Workplace* (2003), I could not put the book down. Barth shares colorful sailing adventures—and humorous misadventures—interwoven with enlightening leadership tips and sensible work relationship rules. This narrative cleverness is probably what propelled Barth's book onto Corwin Press's bestseller list. Marzano (2003) reminds us that stories are more memorable than visual and auditory presentations. So now, when I write, I think about the power of stories and try to weave them into my books. Think about the stories *you* can tell to illustrate the "big ideas" you plan to share with your readers.

Q&A with Elaine K. McEwan-Adkins, Author/Educator

Elaine McEwan-Adkins is an award-winning school administrator, nationally recognized education consultant, and the author of dozens of popular practitioner books. What does it take to write books that people clamor to read? The interview that follows will provide some priceless insights.

Cathie: You are not only an impressive educator but also an extraordinarily popular author. Between your two publishers—Corwin Press and Solution Tree—I counted twenty-nine different book titles currently on the market. That is an amazing accomplishment! How did you get your start as a writer?

Elaine: I wrote two dissertations, one for my Library Science degree and another for my Ed.D. I soon started writing for the *School Library Journal* when I was a media specialist and had several short articles published. My first year in the principalship I began thinking about writing for *Principal* magazine and had articles published there also. But dissertations and articles are not books and I really wanted to write a book. I sought out a mentor and he connected me with the editor of a small Christian publishing house, and my first book, *How to Raise a Reader*, was published in 1987. All of my experiences and passions to that point came together in that book. It was the easiest book I've ever written.

Cathie: Is writing articles the stepping stone to writing books?

Author Profile: Elaine K. McEwan-Adkins

Education
BA Education—Wheaton College
MA Library Science—Northern Illinois University
Ed.D. Educational Administration—Northern Illinois University

Current Position
Author–Educational Consultant—McEwan-Adkins Group

Awards
Outstanding Instructional Leader—Illinois Principals Association
Award of Excellence—Illinois State Board of Education
National Distinguished Principal—National Association of Elementary Principals

Recent Books
(See References for full titles, issue dates, and publishers)
10 Traits of Highly Effective Schools
40 Reading Intervention Strategies for K-6 Students
Collaborative Teacher Literacy Teams, K-6
Literacy Look Fors
Raising Reading Achievement in Middle and High Schools (2nd edn)
Teach Them All to Read (2nd edn)

Additional Titles Listed At
www.corwin.com and www.solution-tree.com

Elaine: It certainly can be. Before trying to write a book, write articles for professional journals, which helps aspiring writers discover if they can actually write for educators. It's more difficult, in my opinion, to write a succinct article for a publication than to write a whole book, and working with journal editors is good training for being able to prepare a book manuscript for submission. If one can't get articles published in professional journals such as *Educational Leadership* and *Principal*, it's unlikely that one can write a successful book for practitioners.

Cathie: There are successful teachers and school leaders out there who want to write for other educators but feel intimidated by the whole process. How do these aspiring authors get past their fears?

Elaine: One way to get past fear is to overcome it with a passion about what one is doing in a specific specialty—a desire to mentor and help readers be successful.

Cathie: In your zeal to help educators become more effective you have written about a wide range of topics—language arts/literacy, instructional leadership, teacher effectiveness, school-wide achievement, parent communication, and personnel management, to name just a few. Where do you get your ideas? What is your mission?

Elaine: In order to write one must have ideas. I get my ideas from voracious reading of both fiction and non-fiction as well as conversations with educators about particular challenges they are facing. Then I link those ideas to my own personal experiences as an educator. For example, the problems I faced as a novice principal in a low-achieving school always inform my writing. I also search out educators who are highly effective at what they do and ask them to share their success stories with me. If I'm going to write about an issue, I want my personal experiences, some body of evidence from peer-reviewed research, and the experiences of others to triangulate. My mission as I write is this: to give educators research-based ways to be more effective to the ultimate end of learning for all students, irrespective of their demographics or the particular labels that teachers and schools have attached to them.

Cathie: Once you have settled on a theme, what goes through your mind when you are in the beginning stages of planning a book?

Elaine: For most for my writing career, I have always been thinking about the next book while writing the current one. In the course of reading, summarizing relevant research for readers, and interviewing educators, I usually had more material than I could use, so I filed it away for the next book. I always pick a title first. Now, most acquisition editors won't let authors title a book. However, I've been very fortunate to be good at picking titles (with the help of a fabulous editor). Once I have that title, everything flows from there. Coming back to that title helps me stay focused on the big ideas of the book. I usually develop a working outline and write the book's preface at the very beginning of the process. I come back and rework that preface multiple times during the writing. It serves as a self-correcting mechanism against losing my way. My definition of "losing one's way" is falling in love with something you have written that is totally unrelated to the big idea of the book and refusing to give it up and remove it from the manuscript.

Cathie: From reading your books—the content, the writing style, and the production quality—I can tell you are a perfectionist. What qualities does an education book have to have before *you* would consider it a best-practice practitioner book?

Elaine: An education book has to have at the very least three qualities for it to be considered a best-practice book: first, it has to answer a question or address a problem that is relevant to the readers; second, it has to be based on a solid body of research in a specific field; finally, it has to translate that research into principles and strategies that actually work in classrooms in schools.

Best Writing Tip

Write, read, and rewrite. All of my published books have gone through my personal rigorous three-step process multiple times. I call it the "click and clunk" method. I read a section that I have written to see if it clicks—makes sense and conveys exactly what I want to say—or clunks—there are spots in the writing that interfere with my comprehension and need to be rewritten.

Elaine McEwan-Adkins

Book Appeal

Elaine's immense first-hand experience in education has given her the unique ability to deliver educator-friendly strategies that are not only powerful but also easy to implement. Her ideas and advice don't just sound good on the page—they translate into meaningful classroom shifts that truly make a difference to students' lives.

Douglas M. Rife, president and publisher, Solution Tree Press

Cathie: The life of a writer seems romantic to some, but in reality it can be tough work at times. How have you managed your family, home, and career obligations in order to leave time for writing?

Elaine: Some authors can carve out time very early in the morning or late at night and have the discipline to do that regularly. I am not that kind of writer. I need large chunks of time to work. You need a passion for writing and a willingness to structure your life around it. If one is serious about writing, one must have an understanding and supportive spouse, and a laser focus on the goal.

Cathie: Writing has been your passion for the past twenty-seven years. What has been your greatest reward?

Elaine: The greatest reward of writing is making a difference in the lives of educators and their students. I love it when individuals come to a workshop with one of my books filled with tabs, sticky notes, and highlighting. Then I know that educators are reading my books and using them to make a difference for students. I love to get emails from readers asking questions about the content of one of my books or begging to differ with me on an assertion I've made. Those responses let me know that people didn't just buy the book and put it on a shelf. They are using it.

Aspiring authors have much to learn from Elaine's passion for writing. Her success strategies are sensible and doable: fulfill a need, research your topic, practice your craft, and be your own best critic.

Take Away Tips

- Book topic interests are influenced by what educators need to *know* and *do* to be successful.
- Helping educators to perfect performance is an important book development goal.
- Teachers and school leaders want practical information, fresh ideas, and solid solutions for work-related problems.
- Sound research includes field tests of proposed practices in authentic education settings.
- A book's format and features should ease readability and bring clarity to key concepts.
- Vivid stories from the field bring "big ideas" to life.

Reflections–Connections

- Do you possess education books that you are reluctant to loan out? What makes these volumes special? Identify the characteristics you would like to emulate in the book you are planning.
- First-rate education books deliver vital information about teaching, learning, and raising student achievement. Are you planning to write a book like this? What features will you include to strengthen your book's message?

Best Practice

- Organize a book study where the participants discuss not only the content of the book but also its layout and text features, like headings, text boxes, and illustrations. What design elements were most appreciated?
- Use the Book Analysis Guide (Appendix C) to critique your favorite education book. Which characteristics will you strive to replicate as you draft your manuscript?

References

Barth, R. S. (2003). *Lessons learned: Shaping relationships and the culture of the workplace.* Thousand Oaks, CA: Corwin Press

Council of Chief State School Officers (CCSSO). (2008). *Educational leadership policy standards.* Washington, DC: CCSSO

Council of Chief State School Officers (CCSSO). (2014). *2014 ISLLC Standards.* Washington, DC: CCSSO

Ellis, A. K. (2005). *Research on educational innovations.* New York: Routledge

Marzano, R. (2003). *What works in schools: Translating research into action.* Alexandria, VA: ASCD

McEwan, E. K. (2006). *Raising reading achievement in middle and high schools: 5 Simple-to-follow strategies.* 2nd edn. Thousand Oaks, CA: Corwin Press

McEwan, E. K. (2009a). *10 traits of highly effective schools: Raising the achievement bar for all students.* Thousand Oaks, CA: Corwin Press

McEwan-Adkins, E. (2009b). *Teach them all to read: Catching kids before they fall through the cracks.* 2nd edn. Thousand Oaks, CA: Corwin Press

McEwan-Adkins, E. (2010). *40 reading intervention strategies for K-6 students: Research-based support for RTI.* Bloomington, IN: Solution Tree Press

McEwan-Adkins, E. (2011). *Literacy look fors: An observation protocol to guide K-6 classroom walkthroughs.* Bloomington, IN: Solution Tree Press

McEwan-Adkins, E. (2012). *Collaborative teacher literacy teams, K-6: Connecting professional growth to student achievement.* Bloomington, IN: Solution Tree Press

McLaughlin, Dionne V. (2015). *Insights: How expert principals make difficult decisions.* Thousand Oaks: CA: Corwin Press

Merriam-Webster. (2008). *Merriam-Webster's Collegiate Dictionary.* 11th edn. Springfield, MA: Merriam-Webster

National Board for Professional Teaching Standards (NBPTS). (2002). *What teachers should know and be able to do.* Arlington, VA: NBPTS

Terrell, S. S. (2015). *The 30 goals challenge for teachers: Small steps to transform your teaching.* New York: Routledge

Book Mechanics and Safeguards

Book . . . something that yields knowledge or understanding.
Merriam-Webster (2008, p. 142)

For which parts of a book am I responsible? Can I embed drawings in my manuscript? Are publishers' guidelines chiseled in stone or do authors have some leeway? These are just three of the myriad questions writers face as they approach the impressive tasks associated with preparing a book. This chapter covers the components that make up a book, publishers' submission and writing guidelines, recommended writing references, and manuscript safeguards. If this sounds intimidating, put your trepidations aside because you will also be introduced to the author's guardian angel—the copy editor. This manuscript prep expert will help you get everything right.

Front Matter

Books are like life: there is a beginning (the front matter); a middle (the main text); and an end (the back matter). But, unlike life, an author can fully orchestrate how well these elements fit together and determine the final outcome. So that you better understand how writers organize their books, we will examine each component separately, starting with the front matter, which includes all of the material that is sandwiched between the front cover and the first chapter. These front matter items are listed below in the order they usually appear in non-fiction books. Brief definitions follow, along with some helpful tips.

Half-Title Page

The first page of a book is known as the half-title page. Only the main title—such as *The Educator's Guide to Writing a Book*—is displayed. The subtitle—such as *Practical Advice for Teachers and Leaders*—is not.

See "Telling Titles" in Chapter 4 for advice about title selection.

Title Page

A book's title, subtitle, author(s), and publisher are listed on the title page.

You will have the delight of being the featured author on the title page unless you have a co-author. In that case, you and your partner will need to decide who gets first billing. For example, will the author lineup read "Veronica Vermillion and Cobalt Blue" or "Cobalt Blue and Veronica Vermillion"? The lead is usually filled by the writer who coordinated the project or did the bulk of the research and writing. On the other hand, the publisher will probably—and wisely—tap the writer with the higher name recognition for the lead role.

Copyright Page

A notice to readers that a book is copyrighted is printed on the copyright page, along with the year(s) published, the edition number, cataloging details, and other publication information. Sometimes editors and members of the production team, such as the proofreader, typesetter, indexer, and cover designer, are also listed here.

A book's publishing and copyright years may not be identical. A book issued in November 2015, for example, may carry a 2016 copyright designation. Your editor will provide the correct copyright year for your book.

Dedication

When an author states that the book was written in honor of a supportive family member, a close friend, or an esteemed colleague, this constitutes a dedication. Equally, a dedication might express a noble thought or a grand idea. In *The Moral Imperative of School Leadership* (2003, p. xviii), for example, Fullan's dedication reads: "To the resurgence of school leadership: This time let's get it right." A dedication is usually the sole item on the page after the copyright page and before the table of contents.

Limit you dedication to no more than a line or two. An overly long dedication loses impact.

Table of Contents

The major components of the book are listed in the table of contents, often simply known as "contents." The contents include the front-matter elements, book parts, if applicable (e.g., Part I, Part II, and so on), chapter titles, sometimes major section headings, and the items that follow the book's final chapter, such as appendices, references, and index. The good news is that paginating the table of contents is the responsibility of the publisher, so authors need not add location numbers for chapters, section headings, and other features.

The table of contents must align *perfectly* with your manuscript, so it is usually the last element to be written. On the other hand, it is not a bad idea to draft the content list as you complete each chapter, so that you can assess the quality and consistency of your headings. Three or more levels of headings may occur in a manuscript: heading 1 (a main topic heading); heading 2 (a subheading under a heading 1); and heading 3 (a subheading under a heading 2); and so on. A table of contents may include: part and chapter titles; part titles, chapter titles, and heading 1s; or part titles, chapter titles, heading 1s, and heading 2s. Your editor will advise you on the publisher's house style, but may be flexible if you express a strong preference for including more or fewer of these elements. For more information about headings, including examples, see Corwin Press's *Author's Guide* (www.corwin.com/repository/binaries/Author Guidelines.pdf).

Foreword

The foreword, which is written by someone other than the author, is a short essay attesting to the value of the book. This testimonial is usually penned by a prestigious professional, such as John Goodlad, the esteemed education researcher, who provided the foreword for *Strategies that Work* (2000) by Harvey and Goudvis.

Finding a notable educator to prepare a foreword would be a stretch for most new writers, but persuading high-profile people to write endorsements is certainly feasible. Endorsements appear on book covers, in publisher's advertising, and within vendor websites such as Amazon.com. Getting an endorsement requires some leg work, so before your book goes to print provide your editor with the names of two or three esteemed professionals. If you are not sure whom to ask, your editor may have some ideas. Potential endorsers will receive review copies of your completed manuscript and your editor will forward their endorsements to your publisher's marketing manager.

Preface

A preface explains why a book has been written, identifies the target audience, provides a synopsis of the content, and outlines what readers should expect to learn.

The preface tells readers why they should buy your book, so don't skimp on the details.

Acknowledgements

In the acknowledgements section, authors thank the people who provided support while they wrote the book. Typically listed are family members, colleagues, and any professionals who contributed comments, research findings, case studies, and other material.

In your acknowledgements section, be sure to thank the publishing specialists who helped in the production of your book. Without these talented folks your book would still be in the dream stage.

Author Biography

A biography presents the author's education and professional experience, leadership contributions, awards and honors, as well as their publishing accomplishments.

Keep your bio to one page, but don't be afraid to highlight your successes. Your readers need to know why they should pay attention to what you have to say!

Lists

The front matter may include lists of figures, tables, and text boxes that appear in the main text, as well as lists of resources and other information that will be helpful to the reader.

Potential readers will be attracted by resource "downloads" that they can put to immediate use, such as worksheets, quizzes, surveys, checklists, questionnaires, and the like. Craft resource documents as you develop each chapter so that the alignment with topics remains solid.

If this front-matter overview seems overwhelming, take a deep breath and relax. In Table 3.1, which outlines author's and publisher's responsibilities for several publishing houses, you will see that many front-matter features are handled by the publisher or are optional.

Do not dismiss the components listed as "optional" in Table 3.1 too easily. Some of these non-essential front-matter elements, such as acknowledgements and resource lists, may be well worth compiling for your type of book.

Table 3.1 Front Matter Responsibilties

Book Component	Corwin Press	Routledge	Solution Tree
Cover	Publisher	Publisher	Publisher
Half-Title Page	Publisher	Publisher	Publisher
Title Page	Author	Author	Author
Copyright Page	Publisher	Publisher	Publisher
Dedication	Optional	Optional	Optional
Table of Contents	Author	Author	Author
Foreword	Optional	Optional	Not Specified
Preface	Author	Optional	Not Specified
Acknowledgements	Optional	Optional	Author
Author Biographies	Author	Not Specified	Author
Lists	Optional	Optional	Optional

Main Text

The main text, which makes up the bulk of a non-fiction book, is *expository* in nature. This comes from the word "exposition," which has multiple definitions: identifying a purpose, clarifying meaning, conveying information, and explaining concepts (Merriam-Webster, 2008). All of these objectives come into play in the narrative of an education book. The purpose of the book is announced, theme-related information is shared, and concept clarification is provided by way of an introduction, special features, and images.

Introduction

Unlike the preface, which provides readers with an overview of the book's purpose and content, the introduction serves as the beginning of the book (Einsohn, 2000). It may, for example, delve into the book's major themes or discuss the research behind the author's assertions.

An introduction might serve as your first chapter, or could be skipped altogether if your preface is sufficiently detailed. Consult your publisher's writing guide and ask your editor for advice.

Special Features

Writers are not limited to sentences and paragraphs when it comes to delivering information. Narratives can be enriched with epigraphs, text boxes, interviews, tables, case studies, and many other illuminating elements. The features you are likely to encounter in education books are displayed in the first column of Table 3.2.

Images

Narratives are also enhanced by the addition of images, such as line art, graphs, photographs, and timelines. The second column in Table 3.2 shows these and other image possibilities. No matter how cogent a narrative might be, without images readers may fail to grasp the author's "big ideas."

Table 3.2 Main Text Examples

Text	Images
Boxed Text	Cartoons
Captions	Clip Art
Case Studies	Diagrams
Charts	Drawings
Examples	Halftones
Excerpts	Graphs
Epigraphs	Grids
Footnotes	Illustrations
Interviews	Line Art
Lists	Maps
Mathematical Information	Musical Scores
Quotes	Paintings
Poetry	Photographs
Resource Materials	Slide Downloads
Tables	Timelines

Back Matter

The back matter appears after the concluding chapter. A variety of items might be placed at the end of a book, such as:

- appendices;
- glossary;
- references; and
- index.

Definitions and suggestions for the most common back-matter components follow.

Appendices

Resource material that may be of interest to readers is often placed in an appendix, or in several appendices. This material might include data displays, forms, quizzes, research abstracts, worksheets, surveys, articles, and document samples.

Resources that can be downloaded via the internet are especially valued. Be sure to discuss document download possibilities with your editor.

Glossary

Definitions of specialized vocabulary used in a book can be found, in alphabetical order, in the glossary.

A glossary will be required only if your book introduces terms that might be unknown to most readers. Computing, science, and engineering books, for example, might include glossaries if the authors use many technical terms.

References

The references—also known as the bibliography—list every source that an author has cited in the course of the main text, including books, journal articles, academic papers, conference presentations, and internet essays. Consult your publisher's recommended style reference, such as the *Publication Manual of the American Psychological Association* (APA, 2006), to guide your preparation of text-embedded citations and bibliographic entries.

All references must be provided in full, but they do not always fall at the end of a book. Some publishers prefer sources to be listed at the end of the chapter in which they appear. Regardless of placement, though, you should create bibliographic entries at the time when you cite the source and keep copies of the original material. This saves time later if you are questioned about the details of a source or need to check the accuracy of reference notations.

Index

A book's index provides an alphabetized list of significant information, such as topics, concepts, terms, people, and geographic locations

(Mulvany, 2005). The editor, in consultation with the author, will determine whether a book's content and style warrant an index. Since indexes require page numbers that guide the reader to the various items' locations, it is prepared by the author or a professional indexer after the book's final version (aka page proofs) has been typeset. See Table 6.2 for additional details.

Some authors leave index generation to their publisher because of the amount of work it entails. However, since the author is almost always charged for index services, you might want to take on this task yourself, if you have the time. Your publisher will be able to provide details of how to prepare an index. A handy guide is *Indexing Books* (2005), by Nancy C. Mulvany.

However you choose to conclude your book, the back matter should never be an afterthought. Drafting the glossary, references, and index, for example, takes considerable time. Finish strong by leaving enough time to create well-developed back-matter features.

Publishers' Proposal Guidelines

In Chapter 5 you will learn how to prepare a prospectus, which is the publishing industry's term for a book proposal. But you should not delay in familiarizing yourself with prospectus guidelines. To assist you, Table 3.3 provides web addresses for seven publishing companies, along with the specific URL (Uniform Resource Locator) for their submission guides.

Writing a book proposal that catches the eye of a submissions editor is no mean feat. So read through the guidelines of your preferred publishers carefully, then turn to Chapter 5 when you are ready to begin. You will find tips and examples that will help make writing your proposal a smooth process.

Publishers' Writing Guidelines

Ideally, publishers' writing guidelines would be engaging, reader friendly, detail specific, and packed with examples—just like the exceptional books all publishers hope to receive from their authors. That is not always the case, however. Publishing is a serious business and some of the guidelines— and the abundance of writing "dos and don'ts" contained within them—are intimidating. Some guides also assume that writers know more than they

Table 3.3 Publishers' Book Proposal Guidelines

Corwin Press www.corwin.com	Proposal Guidelines www.corwin.com/about/publish/html
Guilford Press www.guilford.com	How to Submit a Proposal www.guilford.com/authors/submit-proposal
Heinemann www.heinemann.com	Submission Guidelines for Authors www.heinemann.com/shared/authorinfo/ submission_guide.pdf
Jossey-Bass/Wiley www.wiley.com	Jossey-Bass Elements of a Good Project Proposal www.wiley.com/WileyCDA/Section/id-301917.html
Routledge www.routledge.com	Submitting a Book Proposal www.routledge.com/info/authors
Solution Tree www.solution-tree.com	Publish with Us www.solution-tree.com/contact/publish-with-us
Stenhouse www.stenhouse.com	How to Submit a Proposal www.stenhouse.com/html/submitpropsoal.html

do and neophytes could be left wondering how to fulfill what can seem very high expectations. Don't let these aspects discourage you, though. The publishing personnel behind the scenes are positive, supportive professionals whose mission is to help you—and your book—succeed.

In Table 3.4 you will find URLs for the writing guides of the publishers listed in Table 3.3. Reading through two or three of these guidelines will give you a feel for what publishers expect from their authors.

Should you find these documents daunting, however, the following suggestions will help you navigate your way through them.

Focus on Key Topics

If the amount of material in a guide seems overwhelming, home in on a few priority topics. These might include manuscript preparation details, editorial style preferences, permissions acquisition, submission requirements, and production timelines. Other information, such as digital publishing, author seminars, and video production, is less of a concern as you draft your book.

Table 3.4 Publishers' Writing Guidelines

Corwin Press www.corwin.com	Author's Guide www.corwin.com/repository/binaries/ AuthorGuidelines.pdf
Guilford Publications, Inc. www.guilford.com	Manuscript Preparation Guide, 2013 www.guildford.com/authors/styleguide.pdf
Heinemann www.heinemann.com	Write from the Beginning www.heinemann.com/shared/authorinfo/ authorguidelines.pdf
Jossey-Bass/Wiley www.wiley.com	Manuscript Guidelines for Global Education www.wiley.com/wileyCDA/Section/id-301851. html
Routledge www.routledge.com	Taylor & Francis Group: Instructions to Authors www.media.routledgeweb.com/pdf/tf_ authorguidelines_2013.pdf
Solution Tree www.solution-tree.com	Manuscript Preparation Guidelines for Contracted Authors www.solution-tree.com/media/pdf/Pubs_ Manuscript_Submission_Guidelines.pdf
Stenhouse www.stenhouse.com	Authors are provided with guidelines once a contract is in place.

Skip Non-essentials

You need to know only what you need to know. This includes what you set out to do in your prospectus, new ideas that materialize as you write your manuscript, and anything your editor specifically requests. So you can ignore information about topics that do not pertain to your project, such as how to provide photographs or create line art, should these not be your goals.

Ask!

If you are confused, ask! Editors and editorial assistants are ready to serve. They would rather know early on if you are perplexed about an expectation than find out after you have delivered your manuscript.

Be Detail and Deadline Sensitive

Although publishers support their authors, they don't baby them. Editors are serious, for example, about manuscript preparation details, deadlines, and word-count limits. By the time you sign a contract you should understand your publisher's expectations and already have your book well under way.

The information provided in this book is meant to guide—not replace— the provisions set forth in publishers' writing guidelines. So, become

Author's Note about Writing Guides

Some authors use electronic gizmos—notepads, laptops, smart-phones—to store publishers' writing guidelines. Not me. I like to wrap my hands around a document that will become an essential part of my life. So I print out my publisher's guide in its entirety and place it in a three-ring binder. Major topics like manuscript specifications, permission requests, and submission checklists are sectioned off with notebook dividers. Then I add labeled PostIt notes to the pages I know I will refer to a lot, such as file formats and names, headings, text boxes, and the like. Finally, I am ready to read the guide sentence by sentence, using a yellow highlighter to underline especially pertinent details. Although my publisher's guide is my bible, I have downloaded to my browser's "Favorites" bar hand-books from six other publishers. This allows me to refer quickly to their handbooks if they offer in-depth information about a topic I need to understand better. Routledge, for example, does a fine job of *describing* subheadings, but should I need to see specific *examples* I go to the sample chapter provided in the Corwin Press guidelines. On the other hand, if I am writing for Corwin Press and need to learn more about libel, slander, and copyright violations, I consult the Routledge guide, which provides an impressive overview of the legal calamities that can befall careless authors. Every publisher's collection of writing guidelines has something to offer, so check out as many as you can.

well acquainted with your publisher's guide to ensure a successful—and enjoyable—publishing experience!

Recommended Writing References

You will need a collection of professional-level reference books, preferably those your publisher recommends, such as the style guides and dictionaries listed in Table 3.5. The editions for these references vary, however. Solution Tree, for example, specifies the 15th edition of *The Chicago Manual of Style* (University of Chicago Press, 2003), whereas Stenhouse prefers the 16th edition (University of Chicago Press, 2010). This variation holds true for dictionaries as well, so be sure to consult your publisher's most current guide for their edition preferences.

Note that five publishers in Table 3.5 recommend *The Chicago Manual of Style* (University of Chicago Press, 2003 or 2010), four identify the *Publication Manual of the American Psychological Association* (APA, 2006), and three mention both. Obviously, then, obtaining copies of both of these sources would be a smart move. Not every reference identified

Table 3.5 Writing Reference Recommendations

Publisher	Publication Manual of the American Psychological Association	The Chicago Manual of Style	Webster's New Collegiate Dictionary	Webster's Third New International Dictionary
Corwin Press	Yes	Yes	Not Listed	Not Listed
Guilford Press	Yes	Not Listed	Not Listed	Yes
Heinemann	Not Listed	Yes	Yes	Not Listed
Jossey-Bass/ Wiley	Not Listed	Not Listed	Yes	Not Listed
Routledge	Yes	Yes	Yes	Yes
Solution Tree	Yes	Yes	Not Listed	Not Listed
Stenhouse	Not Listed	Yes	Yes	Not Listed

by publishers is listed in Table 3.5, however, so check your preferred publisher's writing guide for additional recommendations.

There are two additional references you ought to acquire: *The Copyeditor's Handbook: A Guide for Book Publishing and Corporate Communications* (2000), by Amy Einsohn, and *The Elements of Style* (2000), by William Strunk and E. B. White. The grammar, conventions, and writing style explanations and examples in these books are first rate.

Manuscript Safeguards

Once you understand the parts of the book for which you are responsible, have read through proposal and writing guidelines, and have acquired the necessary reference books, you are ready to start writing. But wait! Picture the following scenario before you proceed.

Your book proposal and sample chapters are finally finished and you are feeling pretty smug. The quality of your writing is solid and you are now ready to draft a submission letter. But after hitting the power button on your desktop you get a blue screen and an alarming grinding noise. Panic sets in. If this is a hard-drive crash, you have just lost everything!

Might you lose *your* documents to a technological meltdown? You can avoid computer catastrophes by putting a few safeguards in place. This begins with reliable equipment. If your current computer is more than three years old, it would be wise to replace it; the life span of the average computer is just two to five years. Let's assume, however, that you have a brand-new, state of the art computer. You might be feeling safe now. But wait! Even fresh from the box computers can malfunction. The solution is to invest in a good-quality external hard drive. This device plugs into your desktop or laptop and can be programmed to back up your documents either periodically or continuously. Problem solved.

But wait again! What if you experience a house fire or a burglary? If you lose all of your tech equipment, you're sunk. Unless, that is, you have subscribed to a data backup service. To learn more about this kind of protection, just type "online backup services" into your favorite search engine.

Meanwhile, until you have all of these manuscript safeguards in place, make hard copies, save your files to a flash drive, and store them on another computer.

Q&A with Laurie Lieb, Copy Editor

Another manuscript "safeguard" has to do with the services provided by copy editors. These literary experts help authors prepare manuscripts that are professional in appearance and production-ready. In the interview that follows Laurie Lieb discusses the support she provides authors and publishers, and how her work benefits the readers of her assiduously edited books.

Cathie: Tell me about your work—what does copyediting entail? What is your mission?

Laurie: Publishers or, less often, individual authors send me manuscripts to clean up. Copyediting requires correcting the manuscript with meticulous attention to grammar, punctuation, factual accuracy, wording, organization, and sentence structure. My goal is to recast the text to improve precision, emphasis, and consistency while eliminating wordiness, redundancy, jargon, and clichés. The resulting text maintains the author's content but is tighter, clearer, stronger, and more accurate.

Cathie: Once you get your hands on a manuscript, what's the timeframe for completing your review?

Laurie: Some jobs take a few hours; some take a month. Of course, publishers always want the job done right away.

Cathie: What are your tools of the trade?

Laurie: I'm pretty low-tech. I do most of my work using Microsoft Word (with track changes) or Adobe for PDFs. Some jobs are still coming on paper, so all I need is a red pen and yellow sticky notes. Most publishers specify a style guide, such as *The Chicago Manual of Style* or the *Associated Press Stylebook*; other publishers will send me a copy of their own house guide. A good almanac and the Merriam-Webster *Biographical Dictionary* and *Geographical Dictionary* are essential. My Merriam-Webster *Collegiate Dictionary* is always open on my desk. I also use various resources online.

Cathie: How about publisher instructions—what directives do you receive?

Laurie: The publisher may specify which style guide to follow, mention certain terms that should be italicized or capped or hyphenated, or

Copy Editor Profile: Laurie Lieb

Education
BA English Literature—Douglass College
MA English Literature—Rutgers University
Ph.D. English Literature—Penn State University

Current Position
Freelance (lylieb@verizon.net)

Previous Position
College English Instructor—Penn State University, Utica College

Copyediting Experience
Benchmark
Buoy Point Media
Doubleday
Dover
Eye on Education
M. E. Sharpe
22MediaWorks
And others

warn me of certain problems in the manuscript ("the footnotes are a mess"). At this point in my career, I mostly work with publishers I've freelanced for before, sometimes for years, so I'm pretty familiar with what they want me to do.

Cathie: I know that publishers are concerned about legal issues, like plagiarism, copyright violations, and libel. What do you run into? How do you handle problems?

Laurie: I don't see these problems much. Occasionally I'll query the use of brand names or trademark symbols, but generally I just kick the problem back to the publisher.

Cathie: How do you communicate with the authors you are supporting?

Laurie: Tactfully, I hope, mostly through sticky notes and comments on the manuscript. Most of the jobs I do come through a publisher, so I don't have direct contact with the authors.

Cathie: Copyediting a book is a huge undertaking. Where do you start? What steps do you take from start to finish?

Laurie: I usually take a quick look over the job first to see what's involved. Some jobs are short and simple, with straightforward text; others start with a ten-page table of contents listing not just chapter titles but subheads and sub-subheads. I do a lot of college textbooks that contain tables, diagrams, citations or footnotes, photo captions, appendix, and bibliographies. Once I have an idea of what the manuscript includes, I just start on page one and plow ahead. *Any* word I'm not sure of, I look up. I'm not responsible for checking every factual statement in a manuscript, but if the author has made a point that seems questionable to me, I'll see if I can verify it quickly; otherwise, I'll query it for the author to check.

Cathie: What takes the most time?

Laurie: Probably the most time-consuming part of the job is jumping back and forth to make sure that, say, every superscript number matches the corresponding endnote, which matches the corresponding entry in the bibliography. I keep a running style sheet, listing particular terms that need to be consistent throughout the book (some authors manage to spell a name or word two or even three different ways within just a few sentences).

Cathie: You've edited countless manuscripts. What do authors have the most trouble with—punctuation, grammar, or spelling?

Laurie: Of these three, punctuation, definitely. But that's easy enough for me to fix. The truly troublesome elements are inaccurate wording and syntax. One author referred to "a headless and soulless bureaucrat"—I assume he meant that the bureaucrat was metaphorically heartless or faceless, not actually headless.

Cathie: Thanks for the vivid example of "word choice gone wrong." You mentioned syntax; define it in reader-friendly terms.

Laurie: Syntax involves the careful placement of the words in a sentence—for example, putting the main idea into the main clause, not in a little trailing subordinate bit. One of the great pleasures of copyediting is coming across unintentionally funny misplaced modifiers—for example, "*The Life of Oharu* has been called the finest film ever made about the oppression of women by film critics." Common modifiers like "almost" and "only" can be hard to get into the right place—I once saw in a news article that the actor John Wayne had "almost been dead for 30 years."

Cathie: Even the most accomplished writer can experience "modifier meltdowns." I'm sure your clients are grateful for your help. But what if a writer should disagree with an edit you have made? Who has the final say—the writer, the publisher's editor, or the copy editor?

Laurie: A publisher's editor who knows my work will usually trust me enough to accept my correction and persuade the author to accept it as well. Yet they always have access to the "undo" command on a computer or the traditional "stet" command.

Cathie: Describe the perfect relationship between a copy editor and an author.

Laurie: The author needs to trust that I'm not trying to rewrite or trash the work but using my judgement and experience to make the writing as accurate and clear—and even elegant—as possible. I need to trust that the author intends to express certain heartfelt ideas and merely needs a little help in clarifying them. The third person in this relationship is the reader, who deserves to read clear, clean text without having to guess at what it means.

Cathie: What do you like best about your job?

Best Writing Tip

Keep your readers in mind—how old they are, what they know, what they probably do not know, what you need to explain. For example, middle-aged readers might not be familiar with current teen rock sensations or internet innovations. For readers of a high school or college textbook, Vietnam, Watergate, and Bergman and Bogart in *Casablanca* are ancient history.

Laurie Lieb, copy editor

Laurie: I get a great deal of satisfaction in fixing up a wordy, vague, redundant, or confusing passage so, without leaving out anything substantial or changing the author's meaning or style, I can make it clearer, tighter, and more emphatic.

Laurie touches upon the characteristics of good writing—concise narratives, logical organization, powerful word choice, sensible syntax, and appropriate punctuation. In addition, the publisher's writing and style guides are conscientiously followed. These qualities should be goals for every writer. Take pride in your writing by doing it well and doing it right.

Author's Note about Copy Editors

What do authors, copy editors, and editors discuss? Here is a lengthy email exchange that took place between Laurie Lieb (copy editor), Heather Jarrow (editor), and myself over the spelling of a word:

Author: In Routledge's *Instructions to Authors* a hyphen appears in the word copy-editor. No hyphen is used, however, in *The Copyeditor's Handbook* by Amy Einsohn (2000). Perhaps copy-editor is a British spelling; Routledge is part of the Taylor & Francis Group, a UK publishing firm.

Copy Editor: The name of my profession is one of those words that nobody agrees on: I've seen it written as copy editor, copy-editor, and copyeditor. Ditto for the verb form. The choice seems arbitrary, depending on which dictionary or style guide you use. So since Routledge specifies copy-editor with a hyphen, we should definitely use a hyphen. Does Routledge specify a preference for copy-edited or copyedited? Copy-editing or copyediting? If yes, let's go with it; if not, I'd use the hyphenated version for consistency throughout.

Author: Your questions led me to dig deeper into the *Instructions to Authors* handbook where I found the following in regards to US style: "For US spelling *Webster's New Collegiate Dictionary* or *Webster's Third New International Dictionary* are the standard references." I own a Merriam-Webster's *Collegiate Dictionary* (11th edn.) and on page 276 I find copy editor (two words, no hyphen) and copyedit (one word). Do you have this dictionary?

Copy Editor: Yes, I use M-W's *Collegiate*, 11th edition, all the time and normally I would follow its spelling for copy editor and copyedit. I didn't realize Routledge would make a distinction between British and American style for a word like that, unlike the more obvious distinctions like colour and color. So now I guess it's your choice if you want to follow Routledge's rules for "US style." Basically, as long as your book is consistent throughout, I don't think anyone will complain about which spelling for copy editor/copy-editor we use!

Author to Editor: I am interviewing Laurie Lieb, an experienced copy editor, for my book and we have been corresponding in regards to the spelling of her profession. Should it be spelled copy editor, copy-editor, or copyeditor? From my reading of the *Instructions to Authors* I believe I should follow the US style for spelling. True? If so, Laurie's career title should be spelled: copy editor (two words, no hyphen). Correct?

Editor to Author: Your book should indeed follow US spelling conventions, given US readers are the *primary* audience for your book. That said, in cases where there doesn't seem to be a single accepted spelling, it's fine to go with the form you're most comfortable with. When you submit the manuscript to us, just let us know which spelling you're using (and we will convey this to your book's copy editor to ensure it's kept consistent throughout your manuscript).

Take Away Tips

- Read your publisher's writing guidelines carefully, paying special attention to priority topics.
- Acquire the publisher's preferred style guides, dictionaries, and other writing references.
- Notify your editor early on if you are unclear about expectations.
- Help sell your book by preparing a well-developed preface.
- Heighten impact by keeping your dedication, acknowledgements, and biography brief.
- Visualize each chapter—the epigraph, layout, graphics, resources, and other special features.
- Create useful downloadable resources for your readers.
- Put technology safeguards in place to protect your manuscript.
- Trust that your editor, copy editor, and production team members have the best interests of your book in mind.
- Always thank the people, including the publishing personnel, who supported your book's development.
- Acquire the knowledge and skills you need to prepare a high-quality, professional-level manuscript.

Reflections–Connections

- Do you have good relationships with the people whom you work with, such as supervisors, colleagues, and employees? What did you do to make that happen? How will you build positive relationships with your editor and copy editor?
- Are you feeling distressed by the many steps required to create a book? Think about your professional accomplishments and the substantive projects you have successfully completed. What career skills can you bring to your book project?

Best Practice

- About the Author, in the front matter of this book, is a typical book biography. Use the Author Bio Template (Appendix D) to collect information for your own personal essay.

- Use the Chapter Text and Images Worksheet (Appendix E) to identify the ways in which you might present information to your readers. This will also help you identify priority topics as you read through publishers' guidelines.

References

American Psychological Association (APA). (2006). *Publication manual of the American Psychological Association.* 5th edn. Washington, DC: American Psychological Association

Christian, D., Froke, P., Minthorn, D., and Jacobsen, S. (2014). *The Associated Press style book 2014.* 15th edn. New York: The Associated Press

Einsohn, A. (2000). *The copyeditor's handbook: A guide for book publishing and corporate communications.* Berkeley and Los Angeles, CA: University of California Press

Fullan, M. (2003). *The moral imperative of school leadership.* Thousand Oaks, CA: Corwin Press

Harvey, S. A. and Goudvis, A. (2000). *Strategies that work: Teaching comprehension to enhance understanding.* Portland, ME: Stenhouse

Merriam-Webster. (1981). *Webster's New Collegiate Dictionary.* Springfield, MA: Merriam-Webster

Merriam-Webster. (1993). *Webster's Third New International Dictionary.* Springfield, MA: Merriam-Webster

Merriam-Webster. (1995). *Merriam-Webster's Biographical Dictionary.* Springfield, MA: Merriam-Webster

Merriam-Webster. (2007). *Merriam-Webster's Geographical Dictionary.* 3rd edn. Springfield, MA: Merriam-Webster

Merriam-Webster. (2008). *Merriam-Webster's Collegiate Dictionary.* 11th edn. Springfield, MA: Merriam-Webster

Mulvany, N. C. (2005). *Indexing books.* 4th edn. Chicago, IL: University of Chicago Press

Strunk, W. and White, E. B. (2000). *The elements of style.* 4th edn. Needham Heights, MA: Allyn & Bacon

University of Chicago Press. (2003). *The Chicago manual of style.* 15th edn. Chicago, IL: University of Chicago Press

University of Chicago Press. (2010). *The Chicago manual of style.* 16th edn. Chicago, IL: University of Chicago Press

Titles, Topics, and Themes

A book that tries to be everything for everyone could end up being for no one.

Lauren Davis

When Pat Walsh was editor-in-chief at MacAdam/Cage he reviewed mountains of manuscript submissions. This trying responsibility compelled him to write *78 Reasons Why Your Book May Never Get Published and 14 Reasons Why It Just Might* (2005). Walsh (2005, p. 32) found theme choice to be a major stumbling block for writers and laments: "Not much is sadder than an entire manuscript, whether it be novel, memoir, or narrative non-fiction about a subject no one cares about." So take care with theme selection—it determines whether your book grabs an editor's attention and how well it will perform, should it be published. A well-grounded theme also lays the foundation for your book's topics, title, and the prospectus you submit to a publisher. Sound overwhelming? Fear not! This chapter explores titles, topics, and themes in depth; covers the preparation of the prospectus and submission letter; and describes the role played by the editor—the publishing world's judicious gatekeeper.

Theme Determinants

It goes without saying that an education book's theme—or central topic, as it is sometimes called—should be of high interest to teachers and school leaders. But how does one determine if a theme is sufficiently appealing? You will be on the right track if the theme addresses current education issues—or offers a fresh look at long-standing ones—and fulfills a need. A quick glimpse at a few publishers' new book lists will tell you what is in vogue (Scott, 2014). At the time of writing, popular subjects included: Common Core for English Language Learners, questioning strategies, instructional leadership, cultural literacy, virtual preschools, and co-teaching effectiveness. Looking for hot issues in professional publications is another way to pick up topical themes. Recent examples include: online learning opportunities, school cultures, teacher accountability reform, and "next generation" learning styles. Current books and articles are not the only guides to theme selection, though. Be creative! Choosing a subject few publishers are covering is a smart idea *if* the theme fulfills an emerging need. Some additional considerations to help you find the ideal theme are outlined below.

Goal

Will your book *serve* educators by sharing your wisdom, *lead* others by advocating for a new educational direction, *teach* a difficult concept or skill, or *inspire* practitioners to higher levels of performance? Keep your goal in mind as you home in on your theme. For example, if you see yourself in a teaching role, determine exactly want you want to communicate to your readers. If you want to share lesson plans for investigative science activities, for example, "science inquiry" would be a sensible theme.

Knowledge

Higgins (1990, p. 11) reminds us: "There is no substitute for knowing what you're doing." Don't pick classroom technology for a theme if your tech proficiency is still in the developmental stage. On the other hand, if leadership coaching is your forte, showcase your expertise by choosing that for your theme.

Experience

What has been your life's work? Are you a long-time school administrator, a veteran teacher, or a university program developer? Narratives come alive when they include first-hand experiences, so consider letting one or more of your career responsibilities drive the selection of your theme.

Research

An author's credibility is enhanced when their assertions are backed by survey results, interviews, research findings, case studies, and professional articles and books. Before you finalize your theme choice, ensure that you have access to ample supporting references.

Evidence

Educators are results oriented, and they value ideas paired with convincing data, such as rising student achievement scores, declining secondary school dropout rates, and reductions in discipline infractions. If you sprinkle a few dazzling data displays throughout your narrative, you will drive up interest in your book.

Relevance

A winning theme for an education book is often precipitated by familiar challenges, such as boosting the number of women in career–technical

Figure 4.1 Theme Selection

courses or implementing an educational initiative such as Common Core State Standards. Relevant books that show educators how to overcome obstacles or implement new directives are gold.

Before selecting a theme, solicit advice from the editor responsible for acquiring new books at your preferred publishing house. Be prepared to offer several theme choices for the editor's consideration (the Sample Query Letter (Appendix F) provides an example).

Once you have settled on a theme, it is time to generate chapter topics. This demands considerable effort, but the payoff is a book with substance.

Topic Tips

A well-developed theme requires a rich framework of topics. There are numerous approaches to generating topics, including those outlined below. Pick the process that best suits your cognitive style or develop your own.

Create Categories

You can easily brainstorm topics—and related content—using categories. The following tend to work exceptionally well:

- information (e.g., concepts, theories, definitions, explanations, and techniques);
- research (e.g., professional literature references, research findings, and survey results);
- evidence (e.g., data displays, charts, and graphs); and
- examples (e.g., stories, "how to" steps, case studies, and interviews).

The Six Secrets of Change (2008), by Michael Fullan, illustrates the benefits of using these four categories as topic guides. Fullan's theme is captured in his book's subtitle: *What the Best Leaders Do to Help Their Organizations Survive and Thrive.* He develops this theme by providing: information (e.g., supervisor–employee relationship principles, system-wide collaboration concepts); research (e.g., experimental studies from such fields as biology, business, and psychology); evidence (e.g., business revenue data, student

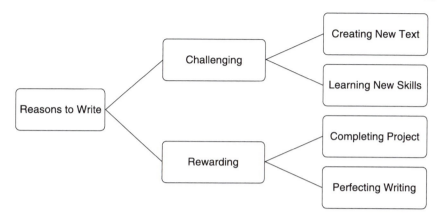

Figure 4.2 Diagram A

achievement results); and examples (e.g., case studies of failed businesses, stories about school improvement efforts). Don't hesitate, of course, to create your own additional topic categories.

Develop Diagrams

Another approach to topic development is to create diagrams. Figure 4.2, for example, shows how a main topic such as "Reasons to Write" can be broken down into several sub-topics. This simple graphic can then be expanded, as shown in Figure 4.3, where the sub-topic "Learning New Skills" becomes the focus of an additional diagram. Whether simple in design, as here, or as detailed as a spider's web, diagrams provide a visual way to record topic ideas.

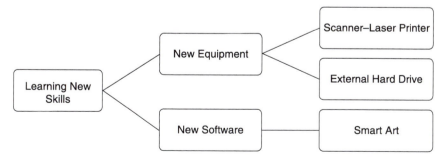

Figure 4.3 Diagram B

Prepare Note Cards

In the pre-digital age, teachers required students to record information for research reports on handwritten 3 × 5 note cards. This basic approach to data gathering still works well for some writers. Ideas and research notes are jotted down on separate cards, sorted into categories, and then into chapter groups. This traditional way of organizing information can be kicked up a notch by using a software program like Excel to generate individual spreadsheets for information categories and handy tabs for labeling them.

Write Freely

Think about your theme and then write down whatever comes to mind for a brief period of time, say five to ten minutes (Nichol, 2014). Do not pause to edit errors or revise the text; just record your thoughts. When your predetermined time period is up, go back and highlight any potential topics that emerged. Irrespective of whether you use this procedure to generate topics, tuck the technique away for future use as it is a powerful antidote to writer's block!

Telling Titles

An ineffective title will undermine even the most promising work, so publishers invest considerable time and effort into naming the books on their list. As Parker (2014, p. 1) explains: "Choose the right title, and you establish instant rapport with your intended readers." An effective title announces the book's theme, audience, and value. *What Successful Principals Do! 169 Tips for Principals* (Fleck, 2005) is a case in point. Merely by seeing the front cover, potential readers immediately know that the book is about—and for—principals, and they are promised numerous tips for successful leadership if they buy it. There are no hidden messages here. On the other hand, a title that is somewhat less descriptive, yet captivating—such as *Living between the Lines* (1991), by McCormick Calkins with Harwayne—may draw readers' interest if the authors are well known. Another approach is a short but memorable title, such as Gentry's orthographic guide *Spel . . . is a Four-Letter Word* (1987).

Figure 4.4 Title Qualities

Author's Note about Titles

The title for a book is rarely a quick pick. In February 2011, for example, I submitted a prospectus to Routledge Eye on Education for a book that would show principals how to engineer best-practice instruction and increase teachers' involvement in school improvement efforts. I thought my title for this book—*Teacher Engagement: How to Elicit and Sustain Best Practice*—was perfect. But the reviewers wanted a title that was more reader friendly. Since I had identified seven key engagement strategies, I added "the 7 keys" to the title and lowered the academic tone by jettisoning both "elicit" and "sustain." So the revised title became: *The 7 Keys to Teacher Engagement & Best Practice*. However, after omitting a low-priority strategy, the seven keys dropped to six. I also incorporated a reviewer's suggestion and worked "unlocking the mystery" into the subtitle; and "best practice" was changed to "school success," because another reviewer wanted the title to identify strategy outcomes. Hence, the title was now: *The 6 Keys to Teacher Engagement: Unlocking the Mystery to School Success.*

My editor, Lauren Beebe, responded to these changes with: "The Keys/Unlocking combo is really clever. I liked it instantly!" However, after consulting with the publishing house's marketing director, Lauren suggested replacing "school success" with "student achievement" to clarify the benefits of reading the book. So the title became: *The 6 Keys to Teacher Engagement: Unlocking the Mystery of Student Achievement.*

By now, though, I had developed some misgivings about the title, which resulted in the following email exchange:

Author to Editor: I am not sure one "unlocks" a mystery. Don't we "solve" mysteries? Or perhaps "unravel" them? But then again I loved the word "mystery" (being an old Nancy Drew fan). Maybe I am getting too OCD about this; maybe "unlocking" a mystery is OK? Gee, this is starting to feel like naming a baby.

Editor to Author: You raise a good point about unlocking mysteries. One normally doesn't do that. I think we may be entering the over-thinking phase of book naming (as with baby naming), so why don't we put it on the back burner until the manuscript is complete? I'm confident we'll have a great title for this book.

A short while later, after experiencing a metaphoric revelation, I exchanged "unlocking the mystery" to "unlocking the doors." So the title became: *The 6 Keys to Teacher Engagement: Unlocking the Doors to Student Achievement.*

This latest revision precipitated another email conversation:

Editor to Author: Because the "keys" are . . . geared towards broader objectives—for example, building trusting relationships and developing teacher leadership—I'm concerned that "student achievement" might be a little misleading for potential readers. They might think the book is focused on the classroom level. What are your thoughts?

Author to Editor: My book shows school leaders how improving teacher *engagement* improves teacher *performance.*

After even more tinkering, the title became: *The 6 Keys to Teacher Engagement: Unlocking the Doors to Top Teacher Performance.* We finally had a title that enjoyed both editorial and marketing department approval, and piqued readership interest.

What did I learn about title selection from this process? Clearly announce what your book is about; be specific about your book's benefits; use appealing vocabulary; and listen to your editor and reviewers, because their goal is to make your book as attractive as it can be!

Prospectus Essentials

Once your theme and topics have been chosen you are ready to prepare a "prospectus"—the publishing industry's term for a book proposal. To begin, review the prospectus guidelines and submission procedures for your preferred publisher. Refer back to Table 3.3 for the URLs of seven publishers who handle education books. If your preferred publisher is not listed, their prospectus guidelines can usually be found on their website.

Prospectus Development

Drafting a prospectus—which involves outlining the book you have dreamed of writing—is exacting as well as exciting. However, it will go smoothly if you have clearly identified your theme, prepared substantial topic notes, determined your book's front- and back-matter components, and selected the special features that you wish to include.

A well-rounded prospectus should specify the purpose of the book, identify the intended audience, list the contents, and provide chapter summaries. An author's biography, an estimate of the book's length, and a writing schedule should be included, too. Some publishers also ask for a discussion of any competition, such as how your book is similar to or different from published books with the same theme.

What should the prospectus look like? The Sample Prospectus (Appendix G) provides a straightforward format for a book proposal, and the suggestions outlined below should be borne in mind as you prepare your prospectus.

Appeal to Your Audience

A prospectus is read by the editor responsible for book acquisitions; independent reviewers, such as education practitioners and academic specialists; and the publisher's editorial board. The tone of your writing should be professional so that the publishing personnel take you seriously, yet sufficiently appealing that the independent reviewers will be hooked, too.

Do Your Best Work

Publishing is a competitive field and the quality of your writing must measure up to some pretty high standards if you are to land a contract. If you have not revised and edited your prospectus multiple times, it is not ready for submission.

Make It Interesting

You are not writing a stodgy book report. Breathe life into your proposal with anecdotes, literary references, and colorful vocabulary.

Brag!

Include a biographical sketch that highlights your professional responsibilities, awards, and honors, such as being selected to present a paper at a national education conference. If you share professional information via websites, blogs, or social media networks, mention them too. Published articles and books should feature prominently. If you have not been published, list substantial documents you have prepared, such as curriculum guides, program handbooks, and successful grant requests. Use your biography to verify that you are a responsible individual who knows how to write well.

Prospectus Submission

Publishers have specific instructions regarding the submission of book proposals, so follow these carefully. A covering letter (see Sample Submission Letter (Appendix H) for an example), résumé, and a sample chapter or two ought to accompany the prospectus. You should submit your proposal only when your prospectus is in first-rate shape and you are confident that you can devote sufficient time to completing the book.

Submission material can be sent either by traditional mail or electronically to the email address designated for submissions. If you have been communicating with an editor, however, they may ask you to send your material to their private email address. Whichever way you dispatch your proposal, good luck!

Q&A with Lauren Davis, Editor

While authors wrestle with title, topic, and theme selections, publishing professionals are waiting in the wings to assist with the development of their books. Editors are literary experts who critique book concepts and proposals, recommend author contracts, and ultimately orchestrate a book's evolution from a smart idea to a sales-ready product. The interview that follows steps into the editor's world and offers writers— both novices and veterans—invaluable inside information.

Cathie: Talk about your job. What is your mission? What are your responsibilities?

Lauren: I'm responsible for signing new titles from both established authors and brand-new or up-and-coming authors. I have to make sure the projects are high quality, meet the needs of K-12 educators, and fit in with our vision and product line. I also help authors shape and develop their projects and guide them through the publishing process.

Cathie: How to become a part of the "publishing process" is of high interest to the readers of this book. What are the keys to landing a contract?

Lauren: Pick a topic that is timely and that is focused, but not *too* narrow. Do a thorough job on the proposal by researching the competition and explaining how your book will be different and fill a

Editor Profile: Lauren Davis

Education
BA Comparative Literature—Dartmouth College
MA English Education 6–12—New York University

Current Position
Editor

Publishing Experience
Editor—Routledge Eye on Education
Senior Editor—Eye on Education
Director of English Language Arts—Amsco School Publications/
Perfection Learning
Editor—Weekly Reader/Scholastic

need. And, perhaps more importantly, know the kinds of books typically published by the company where you're submitting your proposal. If you're sending your proposal to a publisher of books for teachers and leaders, for example, you shouldn't send them a proposal that is written for parents.

Cathie: So aligning book themes to publishers' product lines is a vital goal for writers. What else should authors consider before choosing a theme?

Lauren: Think about whether there's a market for it and whether that market is growing or shrinking. For example, at this point it would be too late to propose a guide to the Common Core because, by the time the book came out, most districts would be way ahead of the implementation stage.

Cathie: How about audience appeal?

Lauren: Pick a theme that will have a wide enough audience. In other words, don't pick an esoteric topic that only a few cutting-edge educators will want to try or that teachers of only one grade level will try. But also don't try to make your audience "everyone." A book that tries to be everything for everyone could end up being for no one.

Cathie: After choosing a theme for their books, authors start considering the topics they want to explore. Are there any pitfalls writers should avoid, such as covering too many topics or too few?

Lauren: It really depends on the theme. If you're writing a practical book for teachers, I wouldn't recommend squeezing in too many topics because then you might not have room to give sufficient examples, templates, resources, etc. for each one. You don't want the book to get too long, to the point where it feels "textbooky" and hard to use. On the other hand, covering too few topics can also be problematic because you want educators to feel like they got their money's worth from the book, such as enough ideas they can really use.

Cathie: Writers would be wise to consult an editor about themes and topics *before* writing their books. Once an author is under contract, however, what kind of support is provided?

Lauren: I offer guidance, feedback, and suggestions along the way. I also send the author's material to reviewers when I feel we need some outside feedback. Additionally, I help the author with scheduling and preparing the manuscript for production. And I am a cheerleader if the author ever gets writer's block!

Cathie: Every author needs an enthusiastic cheerleader. Especially when trying to come up with the perfect book title. Who gets involved in the development of a title? What are the considerations?

Lauren: Typically, an editor works with the author on the title and also consults with the publisher's marketing department. A title should be clear and show how the book fills a need or provides a benefit. It should match the tone of the book—in other words, if the book has practical strategies, the title should feel practical, too; it shouldn't sound formal and intimidating.

Best Writing Tip

Know what other books are on the market and how yours will fill a need.

Lauren Davis, editor

Cathie: How about audience?

Lauren: The title should make it clear who the audience is. And it can be catchy, but not at the expense of clarity. Customers don't have time to guess what a book is about—if it doesn't sound like it's for them, they're usually not going to waste time looking into it.

Cathie: Once a title is selected, what other hurdles do editors face as they guide authors from book proposal to book completion?

Lauren: Some authors underestimate how long it will take them to write the book. Communication is key. I do plan around the deadlines (and our other departments, like sales and marketing, plan around deadlines, too) so it's helpful to know how things are going. I check in with authors periodically and love when authors check in with me, too.

Cathie: Authors and their editors often work together for a year or more. Describe the qualities that characterize the perfect professional relationship.

Lauren: Mutual respect, trust, and honest, clear, communication. It's exciting to see a book develop from idea to published product, so it's great when we can really collaborate throughout the process and listen to one another's ideas and just have fun! Remember we're doing this to help educators and ultimately students.

Cathie: What do you enjoy most about your job?

Lauren: Knowing that my books help teachers and school leaders. I am grateful for all the caring people in education who are working to teach and inspire students!

Lauren reminds authors that marketable books have engaging themes, topics, and titles. These elements are in sync with the book's tone and style and have audience appeal. She also emphasizes the importance of a collaborative relationship between writer and editor. A cooperative author–editor connection lowers author stress and powers up the book publishing process.

Take Away Tips

- Your book's theme and supporting topics lay the foundation for its content, prospectus, and title.

- A solid theme addresses current issues—or puts a new spin on long-standing ones—and fulfills a need.

- Whatever theme you choose, make sure there is adequate supporting material, such as survey results, interviews, research reports, and professional articles and books.

- A solid theme aligns with an author's writing goals, knowledge base, and experience.

- An effective title announces your book's theme, benefits, and audience.

- Your prospectus must be high quality; it should represent your very best writing.

- A realistic writing schedule should align with your production capacity.

- Writing a prospectus is a demanding but exciting endeavor!

Reflections–Connections

- What are the hot issues in your field of work? Could one or more of them become the basis for your book's theme? Will the theme and its supporting topics have readership appeal?

- What book topics can you generate from your career interests and expertise? Make a list of those that are compatible with your book's theme. Can you cluster these topics into appropriate chapters?

> ### Best Practice
>
> - Jot down ideas for your prospectus using your chosen publisher's book proposal guidelines and the Sample Prospectus (Appendix G) as references.
> - Create a writing schedule that will work for you. Consider your work and family obligations and the steps you need to take to create reliable writing time.

References

Fleck, F. (2005). *What successful principals do! 169 tips for principals.* New York: Routledge

Fullan, M. (2008). *The six secrets of change: What the best leaders do to help their organizations survive and thrive.* San Francisco, CA: Jossey-Bass

Gentry, J. R. (1987). *Spel . . . is a four-letter word.* Portsmouth, NH: Heinemann Educational Books

Glathorn, A. A. (2002). *Publish or perish: The educator's imperative.* Thousand Oaks, CA: Corwin Press

Gutkind, L. (2009). *Keep it real: Everything you need to know about researching and writing creative non-fiction.* New York: W. W. Norton

Higgins, G. V. (1990). *On writing: Advice for those who write to publish (or would like to).* New York: Henry Holt & Company

McCormick Calkins, L. with Harwayne, S. (1991). *Living between the lines.* Portsmouth, NH: Heinemann

Nichol, M. (2014). 5 brainstorming strategies for writers. Retrieved September 22, 2014 from www.dailywriting tips.com/5-brainstorming-strategies-for-writers/

Parker, R. C. (2014). Book marketing Mondays: The 10 commandments of nonfiction book success. Retrieved September 2, 2014 from www.bookbuzzr.com/blog/book-marketing/the-10-commandments-of-nonfiction-book-title-success/

Scott, B. (2014). How to select a best-selling in-demand topic for your book. Retrieved February, 4, 2014 from www.articlesphere.com/Article/How-to-Select-a-Best-selling-In-demand-Topic-For-Your-Book/193863

Walsh, P. (2005). *78 Reasons why your book may never be published and 14 reasons why it just might.* New York: Penguin Group

West, C. (2009). *Leadership teaming: The superintendent–principal relationship.* Thousand Oaks, CA: Corwin Press

West, C. (2011). *Problem-solving tools and tips for school leaders.* New York: Routledge

West, C. (2013). *The 6 keys to teacher engagement: Unlocking the doors to top teacher performance.* New York: Routledge

Zinsser, W. (2006). *On writing well.* 30th-anniversary edn. New York: HarperCollins

5 | Writing Style and Steps

Give yourself permission to write badly. And then fix it.

Bob Busk

Picture yourself on a flight to a professional development conference that is several time zones away. You snoozed during the in-flight movie, breezed through the thriller you bought before boarding, and tapped out amusing messages to colleagues until your smartphone's battery died. At this juncture your only source of entertainment will be the airline's well-thumbed travel magazine, crammed into the seat pocket in front of you. Not an enticing prospect, you think; travel is not your cup of tea. But all is not lost because, as you leaf through the magazine, you become captivated by an exceptionally well-written deep-sea-diving adventure. You can't even swim, but you find yourself sinking into the underwater escapade despite your zero interest in the topic.

This scenario is not unusual. Literate adults can find themselves captivated by articles they would have skipped over were it not for the compelling writing of the authors. This holds true for all non-fiction material—from books to blog postings, from essays to news stories. So why do some expositions soar while others fall flat? Style has a great deal to do with it.

Writing with Style

As applied to writing and speech, *Merriam-Webster's Collegiate Dictionary* describes style as a "distinctive manner of expression" (Merriam-Webster, 2008, pp. 1240–1241). *The Literary Dictionary* adds depth to this definition with its take on style: "In the broadest sense it refers to the characteristic way in which a person conceives and expresses ideas through language" (Harris and Hodges, 1995, p. 245). Fair enough, but let's look at two passages that not only explain style but illustrate what it is all about.

From *The Elements of Style* (Strunk and White, 2000, pp. 66–67):

> When we think of Fitzgerald's style, we don't mean his command of the relative pronoun, we mean the sound his words make on paper. All writers, by the way they use language, reveal something of their spirits, their habits, their capabilities, and their biases. This is inevitable as well as enjoyable. All writing is communication; creative writing is communication through revelation—it is Self escaping into the open. No writer long remains incognito.

From *The Practical Stylist* (Baker, 1973, p. 1):

> Style in writing is something like a style in a car, a woman, or a Greek temple—the ordinary materials of this world so poised and perfected as to stand out from the landscape and compel a second look, something that hangs in the reader's mind, like a vision. It is an idea made visible, and polished to its natural beauty. It is your own voice, with the hems and haws chipped out, speaking the common language uncommonly well.

As these elegant passages demonstrate, writing style—the manner in which thoughts are conveyed—is a complex composite of the ideas presented, the structure of the crafted text, the sound of the chosen language, and the sentiments and views of the authors. Style is also influenced by the type of material being written. A doctoral dissertation, for example, requires a scholarly presentation; a grant application a businesslike tone; and an elementary school's newsletter for parents an easygoing approach. How does style play out in education books?

Stylistic Features

Education textbooks, research anthologies, and theoretical tomes are representative of the "academic style," which Nordquist (2014, p.1) describes

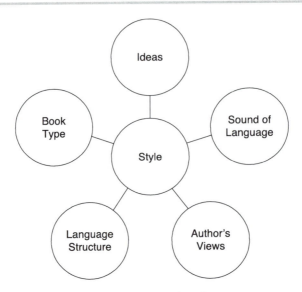

Figure 5.1 Writing Style Influences

as "precise, semi-formal, impersonal, and objective." Academic writing is dramatically different from the style needed for books aimed at education practitioners. Busy teachers and principals want text that is a breeze to read and easy to understand. The author's viewpoint is also prized. After all, the book was purchased because the author had a message to deliver.

This is not to say that all practitioner books share—or should share—the same style. What a bore that would be for the consumers of education books! Fortunately, writing styles are varied due to authors' disparate life experiences, personalities, literary visions, and creative talents. Consequently, educators can enjoy Michael Fullan's bold, assertive voice; Lucy McCormick Calkins's enchanting prose; Elaine McEwan-Adkins's bright, lean expositions; and Roland Barth's colorful narratives. Examples of these popular authors' writing are presented below.

From *The Moral Imperative of School Leadership* by Michael Fullan (2003, p. xv):

It should be clear that when I talk about leadership development, I am not talking just about the principalship.

The pipeline of leadership is crucial. You cannot have highly effective principals unless there is distributive leadership throughout the school. Indeed, fostering leadership at many levels is one of the principal's main roles.

From *The Art of Teaching Writing* by Lucy McCormick Calkins (1986, p. 3):

Human beings have a deep need to represent their experience through writing. We need to make our truths beautiful. With crude pictographs, cave men inscribed their stories onto stony walls. With magic markers, pens, lipstick, and pencils, little children leave their marks on bathroom walls, on the backs of old envelopes, on their big sister's homework.

From *10 Traits of Highly Effective Schools: Raising the Achievement Bar for All Students* by Elaine K. McEwan (2009, p. 117):

The educators in a highly effective school have high expectations, the sixth trait of highly effective schools. They believe in their students' ability to achieve, explicitly teach them how to do that, and convey a profound and unwavering commitment to their academic success.

From *Lessons Learned: Shaping Relationships and the Culture of the Workplace* by Roland S. Barth (2003, p. xx):

We [Barth and a friend] once spent an entire evening relating the concept of "friendship' to the ubiquitous zucchini. Consider the endless possibilities: A friend is someone who, when offered a zucchini, will accept it. A friend is one who, when he has an excess of zucchini, will not offer you any."

Is writing with style a gift? Emphatically not. Style is not an innate quality that magically flows from fingertips to keyboard. As with any craft, it needs to be developed—but how? The Writing Process Actions and Book Development Steps that follow will address this issue and others.

Author's Note about Style

Writing in an approachable manner is not difficult; it just takes a bit of thought. Below are a few ideas that will help you write with style.

Relax!
An education book is not a doctoral dissertation in disguise. Exchange the formal writing you would employ for an academic paper for a more relaxed, engaging approach.

Non-example: Staff attitudes and behavior may indicate that there is workplace negativity.

Example: "How can you tell that a workplace has become *negative*? Does the number of *Dilbert* cartoons tacked to the staff bulletin board provide a clue or does one search for furtive-looking staff members speaking *sotto voce* in hallways?" (West, 2011, p. 31).

Personalize Your Prose
An education book should not be confused with a research abstract. Humanize your message by sharing personal experiences that add color and interest.

Non-example: Some elementary schools have unappealing classrooms, cultures, and student–teacher relationships.

Example:

I was a young student back in the 1950s and my memories of that difficult time run deep—as if I had known back then that hanging tight to what I had heard, seen, and felt would make a difference later. My classrooms were sterile, the curriculum lifeless, and the teachers cold and unapproachable. Their no-nonsense approach to teaching and discipline was so deadening that, despite my immaturity, I knew something was very wrong in my school house.

(West, 2009, pp. x–xi)

Begin with an Interesting Lead

A chapter opening should be inviting. Create an enticing lead by asking a question, sharing a vivid story, presenting a problem, or introducing an element of mystery.

Non-example: School organizations have many components: administrators, teachers, buildings, policies, and procedures. How people feel about their organization is an important variable.

Example:

Think about the word "organization" as it applies to schools. Do you picture hierarchical flow charts showing principals, teachers, and support staff or do you visualize school buildings, playgrounds, gymnasiums, and athletic fields? Or does "organization" bring to mind policies and procedures, rules, and regulations, and the myriad legislative mandates that govern educators' everyday existence? I have learned from decades of experience leading schools that "organization" is not the people, the facilities, or the governance guidelines but a pervasive and powerful mindset.

(West, 2013, p. 21)

Speak Clearly

Words like "transparent" (open), "stakeholder" (constituent), "unpack" (analyze), "piece" (component), and "share out" (i.e., report) obscure meaning for the uninitiated and quickly become dated. Avoid professional jargon.

Non-example: School renewal confusion becomes evident when stakeholders are unable to unpack their school's mission, share out project objectives, or formulate a professional goal piece.

Example: "School renewal confusion becomes evident when teachers are unable to articulate their school's mission, explain how to carry out project objectives, or formulate pertinent professional goals" (West, 2013, p. 94).

Eliminate Words to Strengthen Fluency
Readers may become lost, confused, or uninterested when there are too many words in a sentence. Write concisely.

Non-example: Superintendents and their cadre of principals should create a professional working environment where solid relationships can blossom and eventually lead towards the development of a genuine and effective teaming situation.

Example: "A solid relationship between a superintendent and principal underlies genuine and effective 'teaming'" (West, 2009, p. 45).

Now look at your own writing and determine *where* and *how* you might enhance your style by applying these five simple ideas!

Writing Process Actions

Whether you are writing a school leadership "how to" book, a comprehensive guide to classroom technology, or a science sourcebook for secondary teachers you will need the following process actions. Some have been touched upon in previous chapters, but since reviews are beneficial, every action is presented here, accompanied by some practical tips.

Generating Ideas

A book springs from the themes and topics generated by the author. But there is more to a book than its "big ideas." A writer might choose to add special features like interviews and case studies; images, such as maps and photos; and resources, like fill-in-the-blank forms and glossaries (see Table 3.2 for additional options). New ideas also emerge as a book is being written. Consequently, completed books often deviate from the author's initial vision and the prospectus submitted to the publisher. Changes are acceptable as long as authors have the support of their editors.

A slim three-ring binder is an efficient way to keep track of ideas. Fill the binder with lined paper, then section it off—using notebook dividers—as follows: front matter, chapter 1, chapter 2, chapter 3, etc., back matter, and appendices. Grab your binder when you want to jot down ideas or research notes for one of the sections of your book. Of course, if you are comfortable with digital recordkeeping, set up recordkeeping files using your preferred electronic tool.

Formatting

A book must align with publishers' style preferences, which are spelled out in their writing guides (see Table 3.4 for writing guide URLs). Alignment includes which dictionaries and style references to use; coding options for images, such as tables, line art, and figures; and how to organize the front and back matter.

If a writing guide's description of "presentation style" is murky, check out the publisher's product line. Published books provide authentic examples of format options and text features, such as epigraphs, headings, tables, boxed text, and images.

Researching

Readers have more confidence in an author's ideas when there is supporting information, such as research findings, database searches, testimonies, survey results, and references from current articles, books, and web postings. Expect research work to be ongoing because new topics may emerge that require validation as chapters unfold.

You will need a system for keeping track of research documents, such as data spreadsheets, essay downloads, journal articles, interview notes, and the like. One approach is to create labeled file folders for your book's components—front matter, chapters, back matter—and keep them in a file drawer or a plastic crate. As you collect documents, toss the materials into the appropriate file folders until needed.

Organizing

A book's organization affects its physical appearance, the accessibility of the contents, and how well information flows from start to finish. Determining how to best present ideas and supporting material is a tricky process that requires a great deal of creativity, flexibility, and patience.

Chapter frameworks are a great way to experiment with content organization. Framework development is discussed in the section that follows, along with an authentic example.

Drafting

Drafting, the starting point for every well-written book, allows authors to try out ideas, determine their writing viewpoint, and tinker with text structure and style. Revision—lots of it—is an expectation.

Composition seldom flows effortlessly; were it otherwise, every writer would be published. This is not the case because, in addition to a strong vision, writing publishable material requires a tenacious spirit. But even with these qualities in place writers sometimes feel they are getting nowhere. The words do not come; the ideas dry up; and composition problems seem insolvable. Here are a few remedies:

- take a writing break—your "writer's block" may evaporate if you simply walk away from your keyboard for a day or two;

- revisit your notes—you may find some topic gems that you have overlooked; and

- keep writing—notes, word choices, random thoughts, anything! Even under-par text is better than none at all. You can always revise lackluster prose, but writing nothing whatsoever gives you nothing to work with.

Revising

McCormick Calkins (1986, p. 17) informs us that "revision means just that: re-vision, seeing again." Seeing problems in a manuscript is not difficult if you ask some critical questions. Are my sentences unwieldy—creating confusion for the reader—or do they get to the point? Do I explain my ideas clearly or obscure my meaning with impenetrable jargon? Is the tone of my narrative formidably formal or pleasantly engaging? A practiced writer will revise a passage multiple times until it is "just right." Like Goldilocks selecting the right bowl of porridge, skillful writing emerges from prudent experimentation.

The urge to revise tugs at every passionate writer. The desire to achieve perfection—even during the early stages of a book's development—becomes all consuming. However, this may lead to problems. A book may never reach the finish line, for example, if too much time is devoted to rewriting. Writers can also lose perspective if they pay too much attention to one segment of a book at the expense of others. It is usually best to move on once a section of a book, such as a chapter, has been reasonably revised. However, this does not mean that the author's work is unalterable. Doing a final revision *after* the entire manuscript has been completed makes perfect sense.

Editing

A conscientious editor detects spelling, punctuation, and capitalization errors; problems with grammar and vocabulary usage; and style snafus, such as failing to observe the publisher's preferred formats for the index or references. As you draft your manuscript, periodically take a break from writing to edit. Catch errors early so that they are not repeated.

The references your publisher suggests should guide your editing decisions. See Recommended Writing References in Chapter 3 for additional information.

Soliciting Feedback

Requesting feedback as you write is smart, but be cautious. Find an individual who will offer constructive criticism, but not ghost-write. As H. G. Wells (n.d.) once observed: "No passion in the world is equal to the passion to alter someone else's draft." So tell your reviewers the type of assistance you need. For example, if the meaning of a passage is unclear, reviewers should highlight it, not wade in with a revision. Writers grow from fixing their own deficiencies, not from relying upon someone else's talents.

If you are looking for candid appraisals of your writing, avoid asking family members, employees, and friends. Identify critics who can be objective, understand the type of book you are preparing, and know something about writing. Language arts teachers, communication specialists, and other authors tend to be competent reviewers.

There is no set sequence for the implementation of writing process actions. If a topic appears to be misplaced while editing, for example, the author will revise. But should the author suspect that a vital topic has been overlooked altogether, additional research may ensue. Employ the various actions as needed throughout the development of your book.

Book Development Steps

You will not find a credible "one size fits all" book-writing formula. The temperaments and talents of authors are too varied, as are the types of books they are writing. Nevertheless, the writing steps outlined below will provide a sound foundation. Consider them *suggestions* that should be amended to fit your unique writing approach. You should also consult your publisher's writing guide for additional expectations, since these steps address only the major publishing hurdles. If an action is covered in detail elsewhere in this book, I have cross-referenced the relevant section(s) in order to avoid unnecessary repetition.

Choose Theme, Topics, and Title

See Theme Determinants, Topic Tips, and Telling Titles in Chapter 4.

If you have already identified the topics that will support your book's theme, be prepared for additions as you draft your manuscript. New topics could emerge from an editor's comments, a reviewer's suggestions, new developments in education, or newsworthy events. Even word choice might send an author in a new direction. If, for example, you write that a school leader has a wry sense of humor, the adjective "wry" (devious, perverse) might propel you to discuss the impact of negative communications—a topic you might not have considered previously. When a new, vital topic arises unexpectedly you may add it to the existing text if your word limit allows, or cut a less important topic to make room for it.

Determine Book Length

How long should your book be? Heather Jarrow, an editor with Routledge, explains: "Potential authors should consider their intended book length in light of the specifics of their own project; they should consider the audience of their book, the particular topic of their book, the length of comparable books, and their particular publisher's vision." In regards to word count, she adds:

> Authors often think in terms of "manuscript pages" but these estimations aren't necessarily accurate or helpful in a proposal submission. Given that people use different column and header widths, typefaces, and font sizes when they think of a "typical" manuscript page, it's hard for reviewers and editors to have a clear picture of the author's intention. Word count, on the other hand, is unequivocal.

So how does one estimate word count? You should plan on an average of 245 words per double-spaced page if you are using a serif font such as Times New Roman in twelve point.

Write a chapter or two to get a feel for the number of words you will need to cover all of your chosen topics adequately. Also remember to estimate word counts for the front and back matter, including the appendices. Once you have a total estimate, ask your editor if they have a similar figure in mind.

Create Writing Schedule

The Sample Prospectus (Appendix G) includes a suggested format for a writing schedule. This should be established after considering the amount of material you will be able to generate given your work schedule and responsibilities, family commitments, and other obligations.

Be realistic when you prepare your schedule: if you can write only on weekends, for example, your progress will be limited, so take that into account. And always test out your schedule to ensure it is feasible before submitting it to your editor.

Submit Prospectus

See Prospectus Development in Chapter 4 and Sample Prospectus (Appendix G).

Your prospectus should affirm that you can write well *and* follow directions. So review the publisher's submission guidelines carefully to learn *which* documents you need to prepare, *how* they should be transmitted, and to *whom* they must be submitted. Should you enclose a sample chapter? Yes, if requested, but your publisher may not require one: Heinemann, for example, prefers at least one sample chapter, but other publishers are less insistent.

Obtain Publishing Contract

See Signing on in Chapter 6.

Read Writing Guidelines

Even if you have committed your publisher's guidelines to memory, read them again before starting your manuscript. Double check specifications in regard to typefaces, font size, margin widths, heading style, and so forth. Formatting your documents correctly from the outset will avoid the need for annoying revisions later.

If your publisher's presentation style leaves you baffled, send a draft chapter to your editor to establish if your chosen format, such as your use of headings and subheadings, is acceptable.

Select Recordkeeping Approach

As mentioned above, use a recordkeeping approach that has worked successfully for you in the past. If you are kinesthetically inclined, you will be happy with notebooks and file folders as record management tools. Digital whizz-kids, on the other hand, may prefer to record and store information electronically. Just don't forget to back up your files!

Whichever recordkeeping system you use, keep it well organized and up to date. Don't just throw important documents—research notes, correspondence, articles, and the like—in a heap. Such a lackadaisical approach will inevitably result in the misplacement of vital references, forcing you to devote precious time to finding them again.

Research Theme and Topics

See Reliable Research in Chapter 2.

Although it is important to support your views, an overabundance of research findings and references to other authors' works makes for tedious reading. Avoid cluttering up your narrative with too many references.

Contact Contributors

Comments, suggestions, and success stories from noteworthy people all add interest to an education book. Keep in mind, however, that each contributor has a life to lead—and it is not yours! Make sure you contact potential contributors early so that their material reaches you on time and your project remains on schedule. Similarly, obtain written permission to use names and comments in good time, as the production of a book cannot proceed until every contributor has signed the required release forms.

Draft Chapters

See Chapter Preparation Guide on p. 86.

Write Front Matter and Back Matter

See Front Matter and Back Matter in Chapter 3.

Respond to Reviews

At some point during your book's development a manuscript review may be scheduled. Reviews are completed by impartial professionals from education or related fields who are commissioned to read manuscripts with a critical eye. Review questions typically address audience appeal, topics and examples, chapter sequence, author viewpoint, writing style, title, and special features. Reviewers' comments are generally welcomed by authors who are looking for ways to strengthen their manuscripts. However, do not feel that you must agree with every reviewer's assessment. For instance, although four reviewers love your chapter sequence, a fifth might recommend a massive overhaul of the book's structure. Give every recommendation due consideration, but in the end go with what you—and your editor—think best.

Complete Manuscript

See Submission Essentials in Chapter 6 and Sample Manuscript Submission Checklist (Appendix J).

Finalize Index Arrangements

See Index in Chapter 3.

Collaborate with Members of the Production Team

See Working with Production Personnel in Chapter 6.

Although the foregoing book development sequence appears logical—such as prospectus development following theme selection—it may be advantageous to undertake some tasks out of order. Contacting contributors, for example, might be tackled earlier if you are relying on certain people to provide essential information.

Chapter Preparation Guide

Successful architects are skillful engineers, practical planners, and imaginative artists, and their building designs reflect all of these remarkable talents. Whether you are looking at a school, a medical facility, or high-rise office complex, you will find strong structural frameworks, functional layouts, and attractive enhancements. These same attributes come into play when authors design new chapters for their books. The framework for the chapter is built when topic ideas are put into a logical sequence. Then practical features are added, such as authentic examples, sample documents, data displays, and other helpful information. Embellishments are introduced too, such as illustrations, photos, maps, and other images. All of these elements fit together seamlessly in the hands of a creative and practiced writer.

Framework and Features

By way of an example, the table that follows shows the framework for Chapter 4 of this book: the first column lists the topic lineup and the second column the special features, images, and references. Such a structure makes designing—and redesigning—a chapter seem effortless.

Are you ready to construct a chapter for your book? Use the Chapter Framework and Features Template (Appendix I) to guide your planning.

Table 5.1 Sample Chapter Framework and Features

Topic Framework	Features, Images, References
Title: • Title, Topics, and Themes	Epigraph: L. Davis, Editor
Theme Selection: • Appeals to publishers • Determines topics • Lays foundation for prospectus • Influences title selection	Quote: P. Walsh Book: *78 Reasons Why Your Book May Never Be Published and 14 Reasons Why It Just Might* Year Published: 2005 Page 32
Theme Determinants: • Readership interests • Popular topics • Goals • Knowledge • Experience • Research • Evidence • Relevance	Reference: B. Scott Article: How to select a best-selling in-demand topic for your book Date Retrieved: February 4, 2014 Figure 4.1: Theme Selection Quote: G. V. Higgins Book: *On writing: Advice for those who write to publish (or would like to)* Year Published: 1990 Page 11 Appendix 4.1: Sample Query Letter

(continued)

Table 5.1 (continued)

Topic Framework	Features, Images, References
Topic Tips: • Create categories • Develop webs • Prepare note cards • Write freely • Activate familiar methods	Bullet Format: Creating Categories Reference: M. Fullan Book: *The Six Secrets of Change* Year Published: 2008 Figure 4.2: Diagram A Figure 4.3: Diagram B Reference: M. Nichol Article: 5 brainstorming strategies for writers Date Retrieved: September 22, 2014
Telling Titles: • Characteristics • Examples	Quote: R. C. Parker Article: Book marketing Mondays: The 10 commandments of nonfiction book success Date Retrieved: September 2, 2014 Page 1 Figure 4.4: Title Qualities Reference: L. McCormick Calkins with S. Harwayne Book: *Living between the Lines* Year Published: 1991 Reference: J. R. Gentry Book: *Spel . . . is a Four-Letter Word* Year Published: 1987 Text Box 4.1: Author's Note about Titles
Prospectus Essentials: • Prospectus development • Prospectus submission	Appendix 4.2: Sample Prospectus Appendix 4.3: Sample Submission Letter Bullet Format: Prospectus Suggestions
Interview: • Lauren Davis, Editor	Text Box 4.2: Editor Profile Text Box 4.3: Best Writing Tip

Topic Framework	Features, Images, References
Take Away Tips: • Summary of Key Points	Bullet Format
Reflections-Connections: • Hot Education Issues • Author's Topic Expertise	Bullet Format
Best Practice: • Draft a prospectus • Develop a writing schedule	Bullet Format
References	

Viewpoint

Choose a viewpoint that suits your writing style and subject matter. The first person (from the viewpoint of "I" and "we") is usually used when reporting first-hand experiences. The second person ("you") addresses the reader and is often employed for "how to" expositions. The third person (about "he," "she," "they," and "it") appears in professional writing because of its implicit objectivity. For more information about viewpoint, see the web reference Literary Devices (http://literarydevices.net/point-of-view/).

Copyright and Permissions

When the number of words exceeds "fair use" limits, you must obtain permission to "borrow" text from other sources, including books, internet essays, and magazine articles. Should the word count fall within established limits, you might be able to use the excerpt without permission *as long as you cite every source properly*. Poetry, song lyrics, photographs, art, and tables also require permission, as do people's comments. Check your publisher's writing guide for copyright rules and procedures for obtaining permissions. An additional source is the United States Copyright Office (www.copyright.gov).

Rich Text Format

You may need to save your manuscript in rich text format (RTF) files, which are easier to transmit, open, and read. You will find the RTF option when you use Microsoft Word's "Save" and "Save as" functions. After typing your document title into the file name window, click on "Save as Type," which appears underneath the window. A drop-down menu will appear—click on "Rich Text Format." To remind yourself to save files in this format, write "RTF" in huge letters on a PostIt note and stick it at the bottom of your computer screen!

Efficiency Measure

Authors routinely skim previously written material to make sure chapter formats are consistent and to avoid duplications of concepts, examples, and reference material. Since scrolling through a manuscript on a computer screen can become tedious, consider placing all of your completed chapters in an indexed three-ring binder for future reference.

Task Management

Stay up to speed with time-consuming tasks, such as adding text features, preparing resources, obtaining permissions, and creating bibliographic entries. Completing these responsibilities chapter by chapter avoids feeling overwhelmed when you start to near your deadline.

Q&A with Bob Busk, Principal

Outstanding principals are not just exceptional school administrators; they are also inspiring instructional leaders. Bob Busk, elementary principal at the International School of Kuala Lumpur, Malaysia, is one of these sterling educators. Bob has won prestigious awards for his leadership at the district, regional, and state levels. He has also enriched the knowledge of teachers, other principals, and support staffs by serving as a literacy consultant and teaching classes about the power of

Principal Profile: Bob Busk

Education
BA Education
MA Education Administration—Western Washington University

Current Position
Elementary Principal—The International School of Kuala Lumpur

Other Positions
Executive Director for Curriculum, Instruction, and Assessment—
Eastmont School District, Washington
Elementary Principal—Eastmont School District, Washington

Staff Development
National Writing Consultant—Sopris West
K-8 Writing Instructor—Washington State
National Conference Presenter on Writing—National Association
of Elementary School Principals, International Reading Association

Recent Awards
2010 Administrator of the Year—Washington State Educational
Office Professionals
2009 Administrator of the Year—Wenatchee Valley Educational
Office Professionals
2002 Regional Distinguished Principal—Washington Elementary
School Principals Association
2000 Outstanding Administrator Award—Washington
Organization for Reading Development

writing. In the interview that follows Bob talks about writing competency, quality, and style.

Cathie: Despite demanding school responsibilities you maintain an ambitious blog about life in Kuala Lumpur. Your colorful essays about the Malaysian culture, customs, and cuisine are delightful. How did your interest in writing come about?

Bob: Funny as it may sound, I used to hate to write. I had a professor in my master's program tell me I was a horrific writer! I have to admit I was a bit put off, but took it as a challenge. I wanted to prove him wrong. I wanted to prove to myself that I could communicate effectively on paper. And in doing so, I found my voice. I found power. I found an art form. I found love!

Cathie: There are many adults who don't share your love for writing. Why is writing so difficult?

Bob: Writing is fraught with negative memories. When a child learns to walk, everyone cheers. Videos are taken. When children utter their first words, the words are recorded and shared with Grandma and Grandpa. When children *read* their first words, it is time for fireworks! But what is a child's first attempt at writing? Often scribbles. And where are they completed? Usually in a book or on a wall. And the reactions? "*No!*" A slap on the hand. "You ruined the book!"

Cathie: How about when kids get to school. Doesn't the writing climate improve?

Bob: Think of all the negative writing experiences—writing the thousand-word essay, the thank-you notes ad nauseam at Christmas, the punishment "I will not talk in class" over and over again.

Cathie: Not very appealing. When I was in school I remember feeling intimidated by writing assignments.

Bob: Writing is scary. When you speak, your words disappear into the air. You can deny them if you want. But when you write, your words are down for all to see. You are judged by the quality of your writing. You cannot hide—a bit of who you are is there for everyone to see. Years ago I heard Lucy McCormick Calkins describe how hard it is for people to write. She explained that writers feel vulnerable because all their imperfections are exposed.

Cathie: What advice would you give to educators who want to become better writers?

Bob: Put in the work. There are no short cuts. You need perseverance, grit, determination, and the ability to laugh at your mistakes and look at rejections as learning opportunities.

Cathie: Good advice for the teachers and leaders who plan to stretch themselves by writing a book. What else do they need?

Bob: Background knowledge, research skills, and knowledge of your audience. And voice . . . all good non-fiction needs voice! Also a good editor—a critical friend with an eye for conventions and content. And you need a "rhinoceros hide"—the ability to accept suggestions and criticism.

Cathie: How about writing style?

Bob: First and foremost, read. Read great authors. Read different genres, different authors, and different styles. Reflect on the *style* of writing. What makes it "good"? What makes it "effective"? Second, write; write some more; write even more. Keep a journal. Write notes. Write letters. Follow authors on Twitter. Study! Keep your past writing and compare it to your current work. Do you see a difference? How has it changed?

Cathie: Many authors work in isolation. How will they know if they are becoming more proficient?

Bob: Seek feedback. Not from people who would never hurt you. Find people who aren't your friends or relatives, who don't love you. Ask for *their* feedback. And get into the revision habit. It takes work. It takes time.

Cathie: Self-assessment comes into play too, right?

Bob: Read your writing. Are you happy with it? Can you send it out to the world?

Cathie: Busy educators worry about sustaining their commitments to writing, not to mention improving. Any tips?

Bob: Dedicate time to write. Be true to a schedule. I like a quiet spot where I will not be interrupted. I like all my resources at hand:

Best Writing Tip

Listen to feedback. Was my memo to faculty clear? How many questions did people have after reading it? Was my letter documenting an infraction based on fact and not opinion? Was it accurate? I look at the effectiveness of the message and I listen closely to the impact it has on the reader.

Bob Busk, school principal

notes, internet, books, and computer. I like a glass of wine. When I finish a draft I like to sit on it for a bit and let it stew and simmer. I will then read my work in a different location. Not sure why, but it seems to clear my head and helps me look at it with a different set of eyes.

Cathie: Anything else?

Bob: Keep your butt in the chair until you are done!

All of these are practical tips for developing writing skills. Remember, proficiency comes from perseverance, patience, and practice. Bob Busk is a superlative role model for novice and veteran authors alike; his enthusiasm for writing is enduring and infectious!

Take Away Tips

- Writing style is influenced by the author's ideas, word choice, sentiments, and views.

- Different *types* of writing require different *styles* of writing.

- Academic writing has its place, but not in a practitioner book where straightforward, clear language is valued by teachers and principals.

- A writing style can be developed with purposeful planning and thoughtful actions.

- The sequence of writing process actions—generating ideas, formatting, researching, organizing, drafting, revising, editing, and soliciting feedback—is always determined by the needs of the author.

- Book development steps should reflect the writing approach of the author and the type of book they are writing.

- The word count for a book is collaboratively determined by the author and editor.

- Think like an engineer—and an artist—as you craft the chapters for your book.

Reflections–Connections

- Think about the writing style you want to perfect. How does this style differ from the writing you have produced for graduate-level course work and career responsibilities?

- Skim through the introductions to books written by several well-known authors, such as Shelley Harwayne, Thomas R. Guskey, Charlotte Danielson, and Carl Glickman. Is the writing appealing or off-putting? Why?

Best Practice

- What is it about the following excerpt that makes it inappropriate for a practitioner book: "A pragmatic analysis suggests that while the use of written language is fundamentally similar to that of oral language, the requirements of text-based understanding could lead to an increase in metalinguistic, abstract, and paradigmatic forms in oral language" (Watson, 2002, p. 43)?

- Create a chapter framework for your book. Include topics, special features, and images.

References

Baker, S. (1973). *The practical stylist*. 3rd edn. New York: Thomas Y. Crowell Company

Barth, R. S. (2003). *Lessons learned: Shaping relationships and the culture of the workplace*. Thousand Oaks, CA: Corwin Press

Einsohn, A. (2000). *The copyeditor's handbook: A guide for publishing and corporate communications*. Berkeley and Los Angeles, CA: University of California Press

Fullan, M. (2003). *The moral imperative of school leadership*. Thousand Oaks, CA: Corwin Press

Harris, T. L. and Hodges, R. E. (1995). *The literary dictionary: The vocabulary of reading and writing.* Newark, DE: The International Reading Association

McCormick Calkins, L. (1986). *The art of teaching writing.* Portsmouth, NH: Heinemann Educational Books

McEwan, E. K. (2009). *10 traits of highly effective schools: Raising the achievement bar for all students.* Thousand Oaks, CA: Corwin Press

Merriam-Webster. (2008). *Merriam-Webster's Collegiate Dictionary.* 11th edn. Springfield, MA: Merriam-Webster.

Nordquist, R. (2014). Academic writing. Retrieved November 3, 2014 from http://grammar.about.com/od/ab/g/academicwriting.term.htm

Strunk, W. and White, E. B. (2000). *The elements of style.* 4th edn. Needham Heights, MA: Allyn & Bacon

University of Chicago Press. (2003). *The Chicago manual of style.* 15th edn. Chicago, IL: University of Chicago Press.

Watson, R. (2002). Literacy and oral language: Implications for early literacy acquisition. In S. B. Neuman and D. K. Dickinson (Eds.), *Handbook of Early Literacy Research* (pp. 43–53). New York: Guilford Press

Wells, H. G. (n.d.) Quotation #5117. *Classic Quotes.* Retrieved October 17, 2014 from www.quotationspage.com/quote/5117.html

West, C. (2009). *Leadership teaming: The superintendent–principal relationship.* Thousand Oaks, CA: Corwin Press

West, C. (2011). *Problem-solving tools and tips for school leaders.* New York: Routledge

West, C. (2013). *The 6 keys to teacher engagement: Unlocking the doors to top teacher performance.* New York: Routledge

6 | Publishing People and Processes

Self-promotion is an author's best friend.

Amy Vanderzee

The level of excitement that comes from signing a contract for a book will be exceeded only when you see your name on the front cover. Getting from book contract to cover, however, is a multi-step undertaking that involves the author, various editors, and a team of highly skilled specialists. This chapter will acquaint you with contract provisions and guide you through the maze of processes that lead to your ultimate goal—a professionally produced book.

Signing On

Pat Walsh is the Subsidiary Rights Director at Dzanc Books. "Subsidiary" is just one of the many publishing terms with which you should be familiar prior to signing a book contract. Table 6.1 provides definitions for many of the phrases you will encounter in the contract lexicon.

Table 6.1 Typical Contract Topics and Terms

Acceptance of the Manuscript	Specifies the criteria that must be met before the publisher will accept a manuscript for publication and the actions that will be taken should the author's work be judged unacceptable
Accounting for Royalties	States the frequency of royalty accounting reports and payments to the author

(continued)

Table 6.1 (continued)

Conflicting Published Material	Restrains the author from publishing competing material, such as articles and books that resemble the work submitted to the publisher
Copyright	Specifies who holds the copyright to the book
Delivery Date	Gives the date the manuscript and related materials, such as marketing and copy editor questionnaires, are due to the publisher
Grant of Publishing Rights	Specifies the rights of the publisher and the author in regards to the future use of the book (see Subsidiary Rights and Royalties)
New Editions	Explains the author's expected involvement in preparing a new edition of the book
Options on Future Works	Specifies the publisher gets the first opportunity to consider the author's next book for publication
Out of Print	Identifies the conditions under which the author's book is deemed "out of print" and the rights to the work reverts to the author
Page Proofs and Alterations	Requires the author to identify errors in the page proofs and return them to the publisher within a set time period (Note: Should alterations, other than corrections, be made to the proofs, the author might be charged)
Royalty Rates	The compensation percentages the author receives on sales of the book and for other uses (see Subsidiary Rights and Royalties)
Subsidiary Rights and Royalties	Outlines the compensation paid to the author for additional uses of the book, such as for book club editions, electronic education courses, films, and anthologies
Third-Party Permissions	States what type of permissions the author must obtain if copyrighted material appears in the manuscript
Warranty	Assurances made by the author to the publisher, such as the work being original, lawful, and factually correct

The contract between author and publisher is a business agreement that spells out expectations for both parties. For example, the author is expected to follow manuscript preparation guidelines, observe legal provisions pertaining to copyright, prepare production-ready images, and submit the manuscript and related materials on time. The publisher's responsibilities include applying for copyright registration, providing editorial support, publishing the finished work, marketing the book, and paying royalties. These are just the highlights, however. You must examine your contract carefully for additional details, such as any penalties incurred by authors who fail to fulfill their contract requirements. These penalties could include reductions in royalty payments, fees for legal or editing services, and even contract termination. Do not sign a contract until you understand the full extent of such penalties and are confident that you will avoid them by meeting expectations. And don't hesitate to consult an attorney if you feel you need expert advice.

Can you negotiate specific terms of a contract? Yes, you can. For example, a manuscript's due date is usually agreed between the author and editor. Authors with proven track records might also negotiate monetary advances, higher royalty percentages, and copyright ownership. On the other hand, many an author is content to sign the contract that is presented in recognition of the fact that the publisher is taking a financial risk on a book that may or may not sell, providing free editorial guidance, and picking up the production tab.

If you want to learn more about contract negotiations, two good online sources of information are Writer's Digest (www.writersdigest.com) and the Authors Guild (www.authorsguild.org).

Working with Production Personnel

Publishers' websites are packed with surprising information. For instance, did you know that Routledge published Einstein, that Heinemann is located in an ancient mill on the New Hampshire coast, and that John Wiley founded his publishing house in 1807? In addition to such obscure facts, the websites will acquaint you with their product lines, corporate leaders, and editorial, production, and marketing personnel. Your confidence will receive a boost when you read that you will be working with experienced professionals; and, when the time comes, it is reassuring to see familiar signatures at the bottom of your contract. But do you ever meet these people in person? Well, you certainly might if you visit your publisher's headquarters or attend conferences or public relations events where company leaders and editors are usually happy to speak to authors. By all means make an effort to shake hands with the members of your publishing team, should the opportunity arise.

Once a manuscript moves from the editorial department to the production team, a platoon of specialists join the process. The key players for authors, however, are the high-powered souls to whom they report, with whom they communicate, and for whom they troubleshoot problems. These specialist roles are outlined below.

Editor

The editor, whose duties were outlined in Chapter 4, is the specialist to whom you send SOS messages when you are confused about expectations, overwhelmed by the enormity of your project, or stricken with "writer's block." Your editor also ensures that the final draft of your manuscript has all of the required elements and has been thoroughly prepared. Only then will the editor hand it over to the production department.

Editorial Assistant

The editorial assistant supports the work of the editor and liaises with the production and marketing departments. Their responsibilities include handling correspondence between the publisher and the author, assisting with contract preparation, checking submitted manuscripts for conformity to standards, and assisting the author with the preparation of submission documents, such as permissions logs, pre-production checklists, and marketing questionnaires (Corwin Press, 2014).

Permissions Editor

When an author uses copyrighted material in their manuscript a complex set of regulations must be observed. Written permission to use excerpted material, for example, may be required and fees paid by the author for the

Author's Note about Coding

Pat Walsh has little patience with authors who

> want to skip over the middle steps and move from sitting at the desk with a fetching idea in their heads to the National Book Award ceremony. The serious writer will do the gritty work ahead of time, ensuring a more productive experience. Doing the tough stuff—which is often the most tedious—is what will separate you from the pack.
>
> (Walsh, 2005, pp. 172–173)

Properly coding a book's special features is part of this "gritty work." Since this was my first book for Routledge, I wanted to ensure that my coding met my new publisher's specifications. So I queried Samuel Huber, my editor's sharp editorial assistant:

Author: My book contains tables, text boxes, and line art. Should these items be referred to as "figures" and numbered in order (e.g., Figure 1.1, 1.2, 1.3) regardless of how they are created?

Editorial Assistant: Yes, why don't you go ahead and label all those items "figures" for consistency's sake. If you'd rather keep them distinct, though, it's not too much trouble to have them named separately as "tables," "text boxes," and "figures" ("line art" is not a standard designation used in our books). Either way, do number them sequentially by chapter, so that the first figure in Chapter 1 would be Figure 1.1, the third figure in Chapter 2 would be Figure 2.3, etc.

Author: I like the option of keeping these features distinct. So I will name and code them separately and drop the "line art" label. In regards to text boxes, there are snippets of text, like definitions, embedded in the narrative that I would like boxes drawn around. The production staff will find the following instructions for these "in-line text box" requests: <START TEXT BOX EXACTLY HERE> and <END TEXT BOX EXACTLY HERE>. There are also longer pieces (e.g., author profiles) saved in separate files that

I need inserted into the manuscript. The following directions will identify the approximate locations for these "floating text boxes": < INSERT BOX 4.1 ABOUT HERE>, <INSERT BOX 4.2 ABOUT HERE>, etc. How do these plans sound?

Editorial Assistant: Your coding system for "text boxes" sounds clear enough for our internal purposes, but would you mind clarifying how you'd like them to appear in the book itself? It sounds like you would like the "floating text boxes" to be numbered and labeled but not the "in-line text boxes." Is that correct?

Author: I have coded the text boxes so that the production team can match them to the pertinent directives in the manuscript. I don't think, however, that any of the text boxes need to be labeled and numbered in the book. Do you?

Editorial Assistant: That all sounds good—numbering the "floating text boxes" for production purposes would indeed be helpful, but they needn't be numbered in the final book. And I agree that the "in-line text boxes" will be fine without numbering or labels.

This brief author–editorial assistant email exchange illustrates the careful attention that should be paid to coding, and highlights the supportive role played by editorial assistants. Never hesitate to ask for their help!

privilege. Some publishers have specialist permissions editors who ensure that all of the required permissions have been attained. Others assign this vital task to the author's editor. Should permissions documents be incomplete or missing, the production department will invariably halt a manuscript's progress. So, if copyright legalities leave you puzzled, seek assistance from your editor.

Copy Editor

The copy editor, whose role was introduced in Chapter 3, edits the manuscript after the editor has passed it on to the production department.

Although minor errors—such as spelling mistakes—will be corrected without consultation, authors should expect queries about any significant problems, such as passages that are unclear or formatting that is woefully inconsistent. Respond to the copy editor's queries as soon as possible to keep the book on schedule!

Production Editor

A production editor directs the magicians who transform edited manuscripts into shelf-ready books—the proofreader, typesetter, indexer, cover designer, and printer. Their work is supported by the editor, editorial assistant, permissions editor, and copy editor, who ensure that the manuscript is checked for errors, cleared in regards to permissions, and properly prepared for typesetting. The first and final page proofs—which show the author exactly how the finished book will look—are also typeset under the guidance of the production editor. Clearly, then, their job is highly complex and technical, so it behooves every author to prepare their manuscript to the best of their ability and fulfill every production responsibility assigned to them.

Supporting the Production Process

As the author, you will have a crucial role to play during the production process, and your publisher will expect you to play it well. The typical production milestones—and the author's various responsibilities at each stage—are outlined in Table 6.2. However, these may vary from publisher to publisher—the sequence may be different or some steps might be skipped altogether.

As noted in Table 6.2, authors have responsibility for the all-important task of correcting page proofs. This requires considerable attention to detail. You are expected to spot typos, misspellings, punctuation errors, word omissions, and other "must fix" irregularities (Anderson, 1990). This is not the time, however, to rewrite sentences, move paragraphs, change chapter structure, or add new material. Such revisions should have been made prior to the production stage.

Table 6.2 Production Milestones

Milestone Examples	Author's Responsibility	Publisher's Responsibility
Manuscript Submitted	Author submits a completed and *final* version of the manuscript and other items listed on the publisher's submission checklist	Editor tracks the progress of the author's manuscript, providing guidance as needed, to ensure it is submitted on time
Permission Log Provided	Author provides a complete list of quotes, excerpts, art, photos, and other items requiring permission (with completed permission forms) and a list of "fair use" material	Editor checks the status of permission attainment
Manuscript Reviewed	Author answers any questions posed by the editor, editorial assistant, or permissions editor	Editor and editorial assistant check the manuscript's completion status and adherence to writing guidelines
Manuscript Sent to Production Department	Author acknowledges production editor's messages and responds to questions	Production editor informs author of expectations and timelines, makes sure the manuscript and permission log are complete and properly prepared, and sends the manuscript to the copy editor
Manuscript Sent to Copy Editor	Author promptly replies to queries from the copy editor	Copy editor corrects spelling, grammar, and punctuation errors; checks consistency in regards to formatting and style; and queries the author about any significant concerns

Milestone Examples	Author's Responsibility	Publisher's Responsibility
First Page Proofs Prepared	Author remains available for consultation with the production editor should problems arise	Production editor sends the copyedited manuscript to the typesetter and monitors page proof preparation
Book Cover Designed	Author suggests preferred design elements and colors	Production editor finalizes cover design in consultation with editorial and marketing staffs
First Page Proofs Distributed	Author makes corrections—not alterations—to the proofs following the production editor's instructions	Editor and proofreader make corrections to the proofs
Production Editor Prepares Master Set of Proofs	Author remains available for consultation with the production editor should problems arise	Production editor collates corrections to the proofs and prepares manuscript for final typesetting
Typesetter Prepares Final Page Proofs	Author remains available for consultation with the production editor should problems arise	Production editor checks final page proofs for errors or omissions
Index Prepared	Author prepares index or requests index services	Production editor arranges for index services if needed, checks index for adherence to index guidelines, and sends final page proofs, index, and cover design to the printer
Book Printed	Author supports the marketing contact's activities as needed	Marketing contact informs author of publicity activities

Submission Essentials

Submitting a final manuscript to your editor could be stressful without a reliable "must do" checklist. To build your list, pull specifications from the writing guidelines and submission guides provided by your publisher's production editor and marketing manager. To give you a head start, the Sample Manuscript Submission Checklist (Appendix J) provides an example. Amend this checklist to fit your particular situation.

Marketing

Eventually a marketing manager will impact the life of an author. You may be asked to complete marketing questionnaires, prepare chapter synopses, contact influential individuals for endorsements, or recommend publications to review your book. Interview opportunities, such as for School Leadership Briefing (www.schoolbriefing.com) and Education Week Teacher's Classroom Q&A (www.edweek.org/tm/?intc=thed), might be arranged, too. You might also generate publicity for your book by writing some theme-related articles for professional publications.

Q&A with Amy Vanderzee, Associate Marketing Manager

In the following interview Amy Vanderzee, a highly skilled—and highly enthusiastic—marketing specialist explains the process of strategic book selling.

Cathie: Tell me about your job—your responsibilities and goals.

Amy: I work as an associate marketing manager at Routledge, with a focus on K-12 education. My main goal and responsibility is to get the word out about our new books.

Cathie: New books bring fresh ideas—a valued commodity among educators.

Amy: The goal behind everything I do is letting teachers and administrators know that we have some great resources available that could help them in their district, school, or classroom.

Marketing Manager Profile: Amy Vanderzee

Education
BA Communication—Rutgers University

Current Position
Associate Marketing Manager

Publishing Experience
Associate Marketing Manager—Routledge/Taylor & Francis Group
Marketing Intern—Rutgers University Press
Bookseller—Barnes & Noble College Book Sellers

Cathie: We are living in a "digital world." How has the internet impacted marketing?

Amy: Marketing is vastly different from what it was even five years ago. Traditional methods do still exist, of course—print advertisements and mailers, for example—but digital marketing is the name of the game. Email announcements, social media, online advertising, and our website are the most effective tools we have right now. Who knows if this will still be the case in the next five years!

Cathie: You have an impressive range of marketing strategies. Which do you use when introducing a brand-new book?

Amy: We bring attention to new books in a multitude of ways. Some vital methods, such as new book announcement emails, social media posts, online catalogs, and conference displays, are what people see and notice the most. But a lot goes on behind the scenes as well.

Cathie: What does this "behind the scenes" work entail?

Amy: Our books are presented to bookstores for consideration on a regular basis, our sales team targets specific markets, and our database feeds information on all books out to websites like Amazon, Barnes & Noble, Google Books, and more. This is hardly a definitive list of strategies but it paints a solid picture of what goes on both in front of and behind the scenes.

Cathie: How can authors help your marketing efforts?

Amy: Marketers are working on many books at once. And while we work hard to understand each title individually, authors know their books and whom they think would most benefit from them. When an author shares what is special about his or her book, and why it will impact the market in a certain way, it's extremely helpful. Then marketing can take that information and roll with it.

Cathie: Anything else?

Amy: When an author provides specific people we can notify about the book's publication, that's even better.

Cathie: It also helps to pick a great title and book cover, right?

Amy: A great title catches the reader's attention without sacrificing clarity about what the book is about. And a great cover does the same thing. You want your book to be compelling, but you don't want to mislead or confuse the reader with anything too abstract.

Cathie: In what other ways do authors help sell their books?

Amy: Self-promotion is an author's best friend. Contacting colleagues within your network and telling relevant parties about your wonderful new book are vital to its success. Word of mouth should never be underestimated.

Cathie: How about presentations?

Amy: The books that sell the absolute best are those of authors who are out in the field. They're presenting at conferences, consulting, or doing speaking engagements in schools/districts, or all three! This isn't to say that a book that doesn't have this kind of support won't succeed, but when an author is out talking about their work day in and day out, it certainly makes a measurable difference.

Cathie: It also makes a difference when marketers and authors remain in contact. What is the ideal relationship?

Best Writing Tip

Always write with an audience in mind and direct your book's message to that group. When the book has a clear and focused audience, it makes the marketing process much more effective and the book that much more successful.

Amy Vanderzee, associate marketing manager

Amy: For me, the ideal relationship has marketing checking in with authors—I aim for at least quarterly—and authors contacting marketing with relevant information regarding their books whenever it's available. When authors actively send along new information, it helps us refresh our message and present the book in its best light.

Cathie: You have a demanding job—what do you find most rewarding?

Amy: Disseminating information to teachers and administrators that helps them improve their teaching practices and schools is what is most rewarding. Education is one of the most important fields and we should all strive to improve its effectiveness and success.

As Amy highlights here, authors who view marketing as an ongoing collaborative endeavor will contribute significantly to the post-production success of their books.

Take Away Tips

- Obtain a contract from a publisher before completing your book so that you have solid editorial support during its developmental stage.

- Do not sign a contract until you understand your publisher's expectations and are confident that you can avoid any penalties for failure to fulfill those expectations.

- Review publishers' websites to become acquainted with the personnel with whom you will be working, such as editors, production staff members, and the marketing team.

- Consult your editor and editorial assistant when you have questions, are confused about expectations, or need clarification of manuscript preparation guidelines.

- Respond promptly to questions from your book production team members—editor, permissions editor, copy editor, and production editor.

- Submit the complete and final version of your manuscript and related materials on time.

- Market your book via speaking engagements, interviews, writing articles for professional publications, and creating a website.

Reflections–Connections

- Take a close look at your current job contract. What are the expectations that you need to fulfill? What benefits does your employer provide? What similarities are there between a book contract and a job contract? How do they differ?

- Do you depend upon people in your work world to help you meet obligations? What is it about their services that you most appreciate? Can you provide the same level of service to your book's editorial and production staff members?

Best Practice

- Draft a chapter for your book, observing the provisions set forth in your preferred publisher's writing guide. Make certain you are using the correct software, font, margins, spacing, headings, and presentation format.

- How might you help sell your book? Make a list of three activities you will definitely initiate once your book comes off the press.

References

Anderson, L. K. (1990). *Handbook for proofreading.* Chicago, IL: NCT Business Books

Corwin Press. (2014). Author's guide. Retrieved November 18, 2014 from www.corwin.com/repository/binaries/AuthorGuidelines.pdf

Walsh, P. (2005). *78 Reasons why your book may never be published and 14 reasons why it just might.* New York: Penguin Books

7 | **Conclusion**

I experience conflicting emotions when I sign a book contract; elation is shortly followed by a bout of uneasiness. Why? Because my signature moves my writing proposal from "may do" to "must do." Now there are publisher's directives to follow, an ambitious writing schedule to observe, and readers' expectations to fulfill. So, for a time, I am left wondering: "Can I really pull this off?"

Should you be apprehensive about signing a book contract, let me reassure you—the uneasiness evaporates once the satisfaction that comes from writing something of value takes hold. You also have the rewards that come from publishing a praiseworthy book to look forward to: appreciative readers, professional recognition, affirmative book reviews, and a profound sense of accomplishment. However, if meeting publisher's and readers' expectations still causes you concern, review the author attributes that were introduced in Chapter 1. These are outlined in detail below with some suggestions that will ensure you reach your book writing goal.

Success Attributes

Confident

- Never lose sight of the fact that you are an accomplished professional. Writing a book will become just one of the many challenges you have tackled successfully.

- When you do not know how to perform a necessary skill, such as creating line art, image files, or an index, ask someone who does or search for instructions in books or via the internet. Learning new techniques is stimulating.

Committed

- Whether you choose the hours after dinner, weekend afternoons, or the crack of dawn, stick to your production schedule so that writing at those times becomes a habit.
- Set a daily goal, such as creating a text box, preparing interview questions, or generating a topic diagram. Attaining any writing objective, however small, is always motivating.
- Read research abstracts on your treadmill, jot down chapter notes while you cook, or revise manuscript pages at breakfast. Many exceptional books have emerged from snippets—not hours—of writing time.

Conscientious

- Write, rewrite, and then rewrite again. Revision is at the heart of quality writing.
- Every day ask: "Is my book moving forward?" If you are unable to respond with an emphatic "Yes!" you should adjust your writing goals and schedule.

Courageous

- Overcome obstacles. If writing time has dwindled, for example, due to fading family support, be assertive. Tell your partner, children, and other family members exactly what they need to do to protect your writing time.
- Have the courage to delete even exceptional writing if it does not align well with your theme. This is tough to do, especially if you have labored over the material, but an old adage might help: "When in doubt, throw it out!"

- Learn from your mistakes. If, in your first chapter, your figure labels are out of sequence, your section headings do not align with your table of contents, and your text citations fail to tally with bibliographic references, do not get discouraged. Fix the problems and move on.

Final Note

When I asked Robyn Ross (teacher) and Bob Busk (principal) what they wanted from professional books, their answers were instructive.

Robyn: I look at how applicable the book's topic is to my own personal growth as an educator, if it will directly impact how I manage my class-room or present curriculum. If the book does not hold my interest, I will probably pass it by. There are far too many books available to spend time on one that does not directly impact my craft or me personally.

Bob: I look for books that help me grow professionally. I want to learn from others; I want my thinking to be challenged. As a school principal, books on leadership also pique my interest. In addition, I select books that are targeted to specific initiatives. We are planning our new school, for example, so I am looking at books that will help us design our learning spaces to meet the needs of the twenty-first-century learner.

Robyn and Bob remind us that educators' interests are diverse and never ending. Authors who "tune in" to the needs of their audiences—teachers, school leaders, or both—will produce "must have" education books. Meanwhile, remain confident, committed, conscientious, and courageous. And when you are presented with a book contract, sign on!

Appendices

Appendix A: Reasons to Write

First check (√) the writing motivators that apply to your book project. Then use the lines provided to specify the information you plan to cover in your book.

■ To Serve
Helping others by sharing ideas, experiences, skills, or research.

_____
_____
_____
_____

■ To Lead
Promoting leading-edge educational concepts and practices.

_____
_____
_____
_____

■ To Teach
Teaching complex concepts or difficult-to-master skills.

_____
_____
_____
_____

■ To Inspire
Presenting uplifting stories, strategies, and accomplishments.

_____
_____
_____
_____

Appendix B: Writing Goals Form

First check (√) the goals that apply to you after reading the attributes of well-prepared writers. Then include start and end dates for accomplishing your objectives. Finally, use the lines provided to record your specific goal(s).

■ Stays Professionally up to Date
Start Date: _____ End Date: _____

_____
_____
_____

■ Reads Education Books
Start Date: _____ End Date: _____

_____
_____
_____

■ Strengthens Writing Proficiency
Start Date: _____ End Date: _____

_____
_____
_____

■ Creates a Supportive Writing Environment
Start Date: _____ End Date: _____

_____
_____
_____

■ Makes Writing Connections
Start Date: _____ End Date: _____

_____
_____
_____

Appendix C: Book Analysis Guide

Practitioner Book Attributes	After choosing an education book to assess, review the following attributes. Then look for examples in your chosen book. Is your book a high-quality practitioner book?
Accessible Writing Style	Reader friendliness characterizes the writing style. The text flows smoothly and is easy to read and understand. Examples:
Enticing Topic	The subject matter is of high interest to educators. The content addresses current issues, offers fresh information, or introduces educational innovations. Examples:
Clear Purpose	Lack of clarity is not a problem with this book. The objectives are spelled out in the introduction and referenced throughout the book. Examples:
Useful Content	The "big ideas" are practical and supported by examples, case studies, success stories, activities, reflection questions, quick tips, and process steps. Examples:
Reliable Research, References, and Data	The author's assertions are backed up by quality research, meaningful data, and supporting references, such as articles, books, interviews, and surveys from the fields of education, psychology, sociology, medicine, and/or the neurosciences. Examples:
Multiple Uses	The book is suitable for individual reading *and* for book studies, workshops, seminars, and college courses. Examples:

Appealing Format and Features	Design elements enhance the book's accessibility. Text features include headings and subheadings, bullet lists, keywords, text boxes, illustrations, labels, and captions. Graphic organizers such as charts, webs, maps, diagrams, and timelines clarify concepts. Examples:
Resources	Resources include downloadable tools, such as worksheets, quizzes, self-assessment forms, and surveys. Technological supports include CDs, DVDs, blogs, webinars, website links, and online courses. Examples:

Appendix D: Author Bio Template

Bio Details	Notes
Name *Exactly as it will appear in the book*	
Current Position *Title and employer*	
Education *Degrees, specialties, universities*	
Work Experience *Positions pertinent to the book's theme*	
Professional Responsibilities *Current and past*	
Awards and Honors *Awards and significant committee appointments*	
Leadership *Committees, special projects, professional organization positions*	
Publishing Experience *Books, articles, research abstracts*	
Email Contact Information *Professional or author website address*	

Appendix E: Chapter Text and Images Worksheet

Text/Images	Notes
Boxed Text *Blocks of text within borders*	
Case Studies *Instructive stories from the field*	
Excerpts *Text from articles, books, and internet sources*	
Opening Epigraph *An illuminating quotation*	
Graphics *Charts, diagrams, graphs, illustrations, and line art*	
Interviews *Theme related dialogues*	
Lists *Books, journals, websites, resources*	
Resources *Tests, worksheets, document examples*	
Tables *Data and information displays*	
Timelines *Schedules, events presented in sequence*	

Appendix F: Sample Query Letter

September 24, 2014

XYZ Publishing House
1000 No Name Avenue
New York, NY 00000

Dear [Editor's name],

I am an award-winning and highly experienced principal who would like to share what I have learned by writing a book. My professional writing experience includes preparing program and curriculum guides for my school district and articles for *Principal, ERS Spectrum, Washington State Kappan*, and *Washington Principal*. I have two themes in mind for my book and would appreciate your guidance. Please review the following ideas and let me know if one or both would be of interest to XYZ Publishing House.

Tentative Title 1: *Active Boys, Active Men: What Schools Can Learn*

Every classroom has active boys. These are the eager, energetic males who cannot stay in their seats, whose grades are marginal or failing, but who are "good with their hands." These crafty guys can repair malfunctioning staplers, operate classroom projection systems, and get science equipment—such as bottle rocket launchers—to work. But when it comes to writing a coherent essay, passing an end of term science exam, or completing lengthy research reports they are lost. Without the right supports active boys struggle academically, become discipline problems, or drop out of school. In the right educational environment, however, active boys *can* succeed. This book will identify the attributes of active boys, describe how to create supportive school environments, and provide practical instructional strategies for K-12 teachers. It will include illuminating interviews with active men who "work with their hands" in successful careers as plumbers, construction workers, auto mechanics, electricians, carpenters, and the like.

Potential audience: K-12 teachers, school administrators, and counselors.

Tentative Title 2: *The Power of Teaming: What Organizational Leaders Can Teach Us*

A highly effective organization is the dream of every professional in a leadership role. In the business world, a top-notch organization brings financial stability, employee and customer loyalty, and an impressive corporate identity. In education, a thriving organization is characterized by a strong vision, high achievement, energized staff members, and supportive communities. Whatever the organization, effective teaming between management and staff—as well as manager to manager and staff member to staff member—is the key to success.

Team-building topics include the science behind social behaviors, leadership vision, team trust and values, and communication—the power of listening.

Potential audience: educators and other professionals in leadership roles.

Thank you for taking the time to review my theme proposals. I plan to prepare a prospectus for your consideration once I have settled on a theme. Meanwhile, I look forward to hearing from you.

Respectfully,
[Name and contact information]

Appendix G: Sample Prospectus

[Date]

Proposed Book

The Educator's Guide to Writing a Book: Practical Advice for Teachers and Leaders

Author

[Name and contact information]

Statement of Aims

There are many successful leaders in the field of education who dream of sharing their hard-won knowledge and skills by writing a book. Not a weighty textbook or tedious research tome but an *inviting* book that grabs the attention of education practitioners, explores eye-opening themes, precipitates shifts in conventional thinking, and earns laudatory endorsements from colleagues and professional organizations. Potential authors include elementary and secondary administrators; directors of curriculum, instruction, and special programs; superintendents and their cadres of assistants; and university education professors, researchers, and consultants. The audiences these aspiring authors have in mind are the people who are in the best positions to effect change in schools—classroom teachers and school principals.

But writing an education book that is popular, persuasive, and praiseworthy demands more than a keen interest in helping others. Novice education writers must become familiar with the attributes of successful practitioner books; develop well-researched, compelling content; adopt an appealing writing style; prepare a polished manuscript; and gain the attention of potential publishers. But that is just for starters. Once a writer is skillful enough to merit a book contract, they must learn how to create a realistic writing schedule, meet their publisher's expectations, and work effectively with editors, production team members, and marketing directors. Writing a book is a formidable undertaking, so it should be no surprise when inexperienced writers fail to get their projects off the ground or submit poor-quality manuscripts that discerning editors are obliged to reject.

The Educator's Guide to Writing a Book: Practical Advice for Teachers and Leaders throws a lifeline to aspiring authors. They will learn how to set realistic publishing goals, create theme-related content and resource materials, develop an accessible writing style, prepare professional-level manuscripts, and support each stage in the publishing process.

Special Features

Each chapter will include authentic examples, practical tips, and supportive resources. Readers will also find graphic organizers that outline key points, text boxes that offer clarifying information, and Q&A dialogs with experienced authors and publishing professionals. In addition, each chapter will conclude with three helpful sections:

- Take Away Tips: Provides a concise review of major concepts and suggestions.
- Reflections–Connections: Offers thought-provoking questions that promote self-reflection, career connections, and personal growth—ideal for individual or group book studies.
- Best Practice: Identifies activities readers can implement to apply what they have learned. These activities may also serve as required assignments for book studies and college credit courses.

Competition

The Educator's Guide to Writing a Book: Practical Advice for Teachers and Leaders comes at an ideal time as I know of only one similar book: *Publish or Perish: The Educator's Imperative* by Allan Glathorn (Corwin Press, 2002). However, Glathorn's book is aimed at educators who are planning to write journal articles, research reports, and academic documents as well as aspiring book authors. Too wide a range of topics limits an author's ability to provide in-depth coverage of a single subject. My book has a single, well-developed focus—a step-by-step guide for teachers and principals who wish to write and publish a book.

In addition to *Publish or Perish* I have come across two related books: *On Writing Well* by William Zinsser (HarperCollins, 2006) and *Keep it Real: Everything You Need to Know about Researching and Writing Creative Non-fiction* by Lee Gutkind (W. W. Norton, 2009). However, both of these books cover non-fiction writing in general, whereas mine specifically addresses writers of education books.

Table of Contents and Chapter Synopsis

About the Author
Preface
Acknowledgements
Resources Available as Free Downloads

Chapter 1: Why Write?

Should education professionals consider writing practitioner books? Absolutely! Book writing provides an ideal way for educators to share their expertise with others, fulfilling an important professional obligation. But there are additional compelling drivers: the act of writing provides a rewarding experience as the book unfolds, an opportunity for self-reflection, and stimulating creative and technical challenges. Chapter 1 explores the "reasons to write" in depth, plus author commitment, writing strengths and growth opportunities, technical skill development, and goal setting.

- Interview: Classroom Teacher
- Take Away Tips
- Reflections–Connections
- Best Practice

Chapter 2: Best-Practice Practitioner Books

Reading education books—to stay current, to broaden knowledge, to learn new skills—is a long-held professional expectation for teachers and principals. But finding time to read is difficult for these busy educators. Job responsibilities, after-hours events, and family responsibilities frequently interfere with reading ambitions. The good news is that teachers and principals *will* find the time for professional reading when a book offers information that is both current and practical. Chapter 2 explores these and other characteristics of popular practitioner books, identifies preferred formats and writing styles, and describes the resources that practitioners prefer.

- Interview: Author
- Take Away Tips
- Reflections–Connections
- Best Practice

Chapter 3: Book Mechanics and Safeguards

For which parts of a book is an author responsible? Should the manuscript include text features? Are publishers' guidelines chiseled in stone or do authors have some leeway? These are just a few of the questions aspiring authors ask themselves as they face the daunting tasks associated with writing a book. Chapter 3 covers all of the essential book elements, such as the front matter, the main text, and the back matter. Additional topics include which reference books to acquire; how to interpret a publisher's writing guidelines; what to do about copyright observance; and how to safeguard a manuscript from computer meltdowns.

- Interview: Copy Editor
- Take Away Tips
- Reflections–Connections
- Best Practice

Chapter 4: Titles, Topics, and Themes

Bob Sickles, who at the time was Routledge Eye on Education's dynamic publisher and editor, taught me an important lesson when I first proposed a book topic to him. I intended to focus on the problems school principals encounter on a day-to-day basis, and my suggested title, which I naively thought would be enticing, was: *Trouble in the Schoolhouse*. The supporting topics—which regrettably paralleled the main theme—included such gems as: "Terrible Troubles and Trying Times," "Insurmountable Problems," and "Unrelenting Stress and Sleepless Nights."

After considering my ideas, Bob respectfully—and wisely—advised: "Make sure your writing is upbeat and positive. A book like this could find itself unintentionally descending into pessimism. Please make sure it does not become a eulogy for the principalship."

Conveying an optimistic outlook was just one of the many skills I had to master as a novice education writer. Chapter 4 covers theme development, author's viewpoint, topic and title selection, and reference supports.

- Interview: Editor
- Take Away Tips
- Reflections–Connections
- Best Practice

Chapter 5: Writing Style and Steps

What do the education authors Elaine McEwan-Adkins, Shelly Harwayne, and Frank Buck have in common? Certainly not style; in that respect, these three authors could not be more different. McEwan-Adkins, a leadership and literacy genius, communicates content—concepts, examples, and research highlights—in a crisp, clear manner. Meanwhile, Harwayne's books about writing convey ideas in an attractively rambling, poetic voice. In contrast, Buck—whose specialty is organization and time management—adopts an efficient, no-nonsense approach that aligns well with his subject matter. Despite their divergent writing styles and interests, however, these powerhouse authors do share a common attribute—popularity. Education practitioners seek out their books because their narratives are easy to read, understand, and assimilate. Chapter 5 delves into writing style and also covers critical steps in the writing process.

- Interview: Principal
- Take Away Tips
- Reflections–Connections
- Best Practice

Chapter 6: Publishing People and Processes

In A. Scott Berg's (1979) biography of Maxwell Perkins, the esteemed Scribner's editor who guided such literary giants as F. Scott Fitzgerald, Ernest Hemingway, and Thomas Wolfe, there is a photo of Wolfe posing alongside the mountain of manuscript pages that would become *Of Time and the River*. But this reached the shelves only after prolonged and meticulous editing by Perkins, who worked tirelessly in the background to ensure the completion of Wolfe's book and the author's success. Editors and many other publishing talents toil behind the scenes to help writers craft noteworthy and marketable books. Chapter 6 covers the roles of publishing staff and the book production process itself.

- Interview: Marketing Manager
- Take Away Tips
- Reflections–Connections
- Best Practice

Chapter 7: Conclusion

The conclusion provides additional book development strategies and encourages novice writers to pursue their publishing dreams.

Definition of the Market

Primary Audience

This book is directed at school principals and vice-principals; directors of curriculum, instruction, and special programs; superintendents and district-level assistants; and university education professors, researchers, and consultants. It will also appeal to administrative interns, teachers on special assignments, and other educators in leadership roles who have writing aspirations.

Secondary Audience

Other readers—and potential authors—include university and college instructors who teach courses related to education, such as psychology, sociology, philosophy, and social-behavioral science.

Course Adoptions

The book provides ideal material for workshops, book studies, and university courses, especially those covering book writing and publishing.

Word Count and Writing Schedule

The manuscript will run between 30,000 and 35,000 words. The anticipated completion schedule follows:

- June 2014: Chapters 1–2
- August 2014: Chapters 3–4
- October 2014: Chapters 5–6
- December 2014: Chapter 7
- January 2015: Front Matter
- February 2015: Back Matter, including Appendices and Index

About the Author

[Biographical information]

Reference

Berg, A. S. (1979). *Max Perkins: Editor of genius.* London: Hamish Hamilton

Appendix H: Sample Submission Letter

October 1, 2014
XYZ Publishing House
1000 No Name Avenue
New York, NY 00000

Dear [Editor's name],

I am a highly experienced mathematics coach who serves students and staff in a school district that has earned prestigious awards for driving up student achievement. I am submitting a prospectus for an instructional guide for elementary and secondary teachers that presents a step-by-step process for improving students' mathematics proficiency. My book is titled *Math on the Upswing: 12 Teaching Steps that Work!*

My writing experience includes a *Gr. K -12 Mathematics Curriculum Guide*, a student handbook called *Math Tips*, a monthly newsletter for parents titled *Math Links*, and several articles that have appeared in *Mathematics Today*, an international journal for secondary- and university-level mathematics teachers.

In addition to this letter you will find my prospectus, two sample chapters, and my curriculum vitae. Please let me know if you need any additional information. Meanwhile, thank you for taking the time to review my book proposal.

Respectfully,
[Name and contact information]

Appendix I: Chapter Framework and Features Template

Topic Framework	Features and Images
Chapter Title:	
Topic 1: Details:	
Topic 2: Details:	
Topic 3: Details:	
Topic 4: Details:	
Topic 5: Details:	
Topic 6: Details:	
Summary:	
Application Opportunities:	
References:	

Appendix J: Sample Manuscript Submission Checklist

Provide Contact Information

- Name
- Mailing address
- Physical address
- Home phone/cell
- Business phone/cell
- Email address

Prepare Manuscript

- Style guide utilized: *Publication Manual of the American Psychological Association*
- Spelling style: US
- Font: Times New Roman
- Spacing: double spaced
- Saved in: Rich Text Format
- Headings: Word Style Gallery Heading 1, Heading 2, Heading 3
- Margins: 1 inch top, bottom, sides
- Pagination: main text numbered consecutively
- Half-title page
- Title page
- Dedication
- Contents
- Author biography
- Preface
- Acknowledgements
- Main chapters
- Conclusion

- Separate files: text boxes, figures, tables
- Call-outs: boxed text, text boxes, figures, tables
- Appendices: letter codes
- Main text citations
- References: by chapter

Check Quality

- Spelling and grammar check activated
- Chapter formatting and special features consistent
- Text citations properly prepared and complete
- References properly prepared and complete
- Examples and resources provided

Document Permissions

- Permissions log for copyrighted material
- Log of "fair use" material
- Signed permissions forms

Complete Other Requirements

- Production department checklist
- Writer's guide checklist
- Index arrangements
- Final word count
- Marketing online survey
- Chapter abstracts
- Copy editor notes
- Art log

- Captions: text boxes, figures, tables
- Numbers: text boxes, figures, tables
- Cover suggestions
- Endorsement recommendations

Index

Page numbers in bold denote figures or tables.